Learn to Play
PIANO
IN SIX WEEKS OR LESS

Intermediate Level

Learn to Play
PIANO
IN SIX WEEKS OR LESS

Intermediate Level

DAN DELANEY & BILL CHOTKOWSKI

STERLING
New York

STERLING
New York

An Imprint of Sterling Publishing, Co., Inc.
1166 Avenue of the Americas
New York, NY 10016

ISBN 978-1-4549-3231-4

Distributed in Canada by Sterling Publishing Co., Inc.
c/o Canadian Manda Group, 664 Annette Street
Toronto, Ontario M6S 2C8, Canada
Distributed in the United Kingdom by GMC Distribution Services
Castle Place, 166 High Street, Lewes, East Sussex BN7 1XU, England
Distributed in Australia by NewSouth Books
University of New South Wales, Sydney, NSW 2052, Australia

For information about custom editions, special sales, and premium and corporate purchases,
please contact Sterling Special Sales at 800-805-5489 or specialsales@sterlingpublishing.com.

Manufactured in China

2 4 6 8 10 9 7 5 3 1

sterlingpublishing.com

Cover design by Gina Bonanno

Contents

Preface by Bill Chotkowski

Ifirst met Dan Delaney while creating a software package of video piano lessons in 1995, and I soon asked him to be my content expert. My company, Abaco, was developing software titles to be used at home on topics like piano, cooking, exercise, running and training, and career improvement. Little did I know that Dan and I would still be working together twenty-three years later. We have become great friends and great collaborators. Along the way, we have introduced the piano to hundreds of thousands of people worldwide.

I've spent my career making computers useful to ordinary people. When I was a student at MIT, I was one of a handful of students looking into the usability of computers: how the "man or woman on the street" would use a computer. At the time, computers were expensive, not yet affordable enough for personal use. Nearly everyone else at MIT was using computers to crunch numbers and assist in the design of buildings, bridges, airplanes, and whatever else they could think of. What interested me was how we could modify our technologies so that in the future, using a personal computer would become as commonplace as reading a book.

Well, thanks to that original handful at MIT, that future has arrived, and we have contributed in positive ways to everyone's use of computers in all aspects of everyday life. Along the way, I learned to observe how people understood things and how to design software for novices as well as experts. I learned that I needed to take into account how people understood the particular topic presented in that computer software—whether it was cooking, exercise, or piano. I tried to design every button, prompt, menu, and graphic so that novices and experts alike could use it effortlessly. It turned out that this skill applied not only to interactive computer software, but to everything else I touched as well.

This experience led me to write a beginners' piano book with Dan, *Learn to Play Piano in Six Weeks or Less*. The success of our first book has led to the creation of this second book, aimed at piano players who want to take their playing to the next level. To create the book, we first defined its goal. We wanted a book that would teach piano players a cohesive set of advanced techniques, allowing them to take any lead sheet and play it with a full rich sound, and even apply some of their own interpretation to the music. Because Dan could teach you new piano ideas for the rest of your life, distilling his lessons into a six-week set took a lot of thought.

After we decided on the goal, Dan designed the lessons, created all the sheet music, and shot videos of himself teaching all the lessons. Dan has been creating videos since the early nineties, when his delivery method was Betamax tapes through the mail. *Keyboard* magazine praised him as a pioneer back then, and he has pioneered with new technology throughout the years. Dan and I introduced online streaming videos in 2003, before anyone had heard of YouTube. Now he streams videos on the Internet, creating them in a multi-camera studio and editing them with Apple's Final Cut Pro.

Using Dan's videos and sheet music, I created the graphics for the book to help illustrate what he is teaching. I incorporated all of his instructions from the videos into the text of the book, adding the graphics for reference. So even though I *wrote* the text found on these pages, the words *originated* in Dan's videos. We decided to present them informally, as though Dan were sitting beside you at the keyboard, giving you the lesson. We also decided to provide you with free access to the online videos to really personalize the presentation of the material. The combination of this book and the videos is a powerful solution that you will enjoy. It allows you to virtually visit Dan any day of the year.

We feel that we have achieved our purpose. We have designed piano techniques that can be learned quickly and used by intermediate players to get to higher levels of playing. These techniques are used by the pros; they are both a solid and enjoyable method of playing and a foundation for moving into more advanced skill sets. They will give you a lifetime of enjoyable music, either as presented or as the foundation of higher levels of playing.

I hope you enjoy these six weeks. After the last page, I hope you will agree that this is the best book of piano lessons you have ever seen. Have fun!

—Bill Chotkowski

Foreword by Dan Delaney

I began playing the piano as a young kid. I knew from a very early age that I wanted to become a professional pianist. At the age of 16, I began my private teaching practice and drove to students' homes, allowing fifteen minutes between the lessons. Eager to further pursue my dream, I enrolled in Berklee College of Music in Boston while still attending high school. This initial exposure prepared me for what was to come of my world and my contribution to music. I continued at Berklee College of Music following high school, and my experience allowed me to network quickly. Opportunities soon began to unfold.

In 1975, after attending Berklee, I studied extensively with notable jazz educators Dick Odgren, Paul Schmeiling, Harvey Diamond, and Charlie Banacos. While I was in Boston I was very active in the jazz scene and through the years have performed with many inspiring jazz artists.

I began teaching piano by video correspondence in 1989. I was acknowledged as a pioneer in teaching by *Keyboard* magazine, television, and other media. Back then, videos meant Betamax tapes delivered through the US mail. I continued to push new video technologies and began to stream videos on the Internet in 2003, long before YouTube was a common name. Now I have a multi-camera video studio and edit the final videos using Apple's Final Cut Pro. My unique experience of years of video-based piano instruction, advanced video editing, and combining videos with book lessons enables me to provide a powerful solution to you.

Along with being a video instructor, I continued to expand my career in other areas as well. I assisted in the start of the Mountaintop Music School, developed a software product with Abaco Software, played at the Ritz, the Four Seasons, and the Phoenician, taught at two colleges, did some recording projects, published a book, and was included in the Earthworks Microphones Artists group.

Here I am, forty-five years after I first began teaching. I feel blessed to be able to say that every day, I love what I do. I find myself fueled with decades of experience and more committed than ever to my teaching, continually writing and performing regularly. This dedication and years of experience have helped me refine my very own comprehensive and unique method for teaching piano, jazz improvisation, and harmony.

I can confidently say that upon completing my Intermediate version of *Learn to Play Piano in Six Weeks or Less*, you will find yourself in a wonderful place musically. You will have developed a complete and solid foundation to enjoy now, and to build upon as you continue with your playing.

Be patient: it will be well worth your efforts . . . and sooner than you think possible.

—Dan Delaney

How to Use This Book

*L*earn to Play Piano in Six Weeks or Less: Intermediate Level consists of 40 lessons divided into six weeks of instructions. As you go through the book, you should cover all the lessons of a given week at the same time. I recommend this because our lesson topics support each other: what you learn in one lesson reinforces the others. Spend five to ten minutes on each lesson during each sitting in the week, until you are comfortable with all the techniques, and then move on to the next week. Daily exposure is best; even just five minutes a day will promote the successful growth of your skills.

Each week suggests a tune to play. These tunes can be played at different levels of complexity, using the techniques that are learned throughout the book. Each week, you can play any of the six tunes; just make sure you are playing the tune at a level that incorporates only the techniques that you have mastered.

Videos of Dan Playing the Entire Book: Free

Learn to Play Piano in Six Weeks or Less: Intermediate Level is augmented by free online streaming videos supplied at Pianoinstruction.com. I am supplying them for free because the videos are a valuable aid to mastering every lesson in the book. I want you to succeed. All you need to do is register at the site to access the videos. The videos are high-definition, and each is approximately ten minutes long.

In each video, I teach one of the lessons. Even though the book is designed to be all you need to master the lessons, the complement of hearing and watching me instruct and play the lessons gives you valuable audio and visual information. The videos let you see and hear how a lesson should be played, and your ears can tell you when you are playing the lesson correctly. Students in traditional piano lessons often have to rely on their memory to recall lesson content; now you have the ability to watch me play the entire lesson at any time at exactly your level to assure your complete success. Using the videos is like having me in your home, helping you any night of the week.

Six Topics

The book has six basic topics of instructions (Shells, Patterns, Stride, Diatonic Improvisation, 3rds, and Blues), and a portion of each topic appears as a lesson every week. Each lesson explains a technique, and then reinforces that technique with a set of exercises in a worksheet at the end of the lesson. These exercises help make the skills second nature, committing them to memory so they can be introduced into tunes as you play. As you progress through the book, you will find that the techniques are easier and easier to apply. This applies even in the months after completing the book. You will become more facile the more you play.

If you do find that a certain technique gives you problems, even months down the road, you can return to the lesson and exercise the skill again until you are comfortable. The exercises help you find your playing options quickly, and typically that agility is what is needed to play the techniques smoothly.

Each person using this book comes with a different background of playing experience. There are a few basics that are needed that we have chosen to put into the appendix. These basics will also be backed up by free videos on **www.pianoinstruction.com**. You may or may not need to use these lessons to get up to speed, but they are available if necessary.

Instructions, Videos, and Worksheets

At the start of each lesson, you should first spend your time with the book at the piano, going through the explanation of a technique and understanding it by playing the 1 and 2 line examples attached to the explanation. Supplement this by watching the videos at your computer (there is no need to bring the computer to your piano).

As the week progresses, your time will increasingly be spent at the piano playing through the worksheets that are provided at the end of each lesson. These sessions with the worksheets will help make each technique second nature.

Introduction

Welcome to *Learn to Play Piano in Six Weeks or Less: Intermediate Level*. I am going to show you how to progress to the next level of playing. You are about to learn professional skills based on open-chord harmony spread out between two hands. These are techniques that you will enjoy for the rest of your life.

My book is designed to bring playing your favorite tunes to another level, using lead sheets and fake books. Lead sheets and fake books are affordable music sheets composed of a treble clef melody and chords. They are used all the time by professional players. When you have gone through the book, you will be well versed at playing your favorite tunes with professional techniques. Of course, you won't be ready for a gig at your local restaurant or jazz club, but you will be ready to enjoy yourself with your favorite fake book and show off to all your friends. You will be well based, and your playing will get better and better as you apply your new skills to your tunes. You will also be ready for adding on other advanced techniques, because you will have mastered an important foundation of professional skills.

Who Can Use This Book?

This book can be used by anyone with a basic knowledge of the piano. Certainly those players who have used my *Learn to Play Piano in Six Weeks or Less* will be able to jump right in. Players with knowledge of chords can quickly grasp our shell techniques and progress through the book. Traditional bass clef and treble clef readers will need to learn about chords and shells, but often these players have other piano skills that they can bring to bear in succeeding with the book. I have included a few lessons in the appendices that will help players of all kinds understand the foundation pieces that they need to start enjoying the book.

The Chord Method

I teach a method of chords in the left hand and treble clef-based tunes in the right hand. I will teach you not just chords, but all the tones of a chord and how to spread them across both hands. These are all professional techniques, and you can see and hear them used every day at restaurants, piano bars, and clubs around the world. If you are at dinner with a friend, and there is a piano player in the background playing show tunes, movie tunes, slow jazz, and other popular pieces, most likely that player's skills are based on the same professional techniques that are presented in this book. This book won't show you how to play a symphony or other classical piano piece—although there are fake books for classical pieces that present the music in lead sheet format. This book's focus is on popular modern, lead sheet, chord/tune-based piano.

Free Online Videos

All the lessons in the book are supplemented with free online videos supplied at **www.pianoinstruction.com**, videos that were created expressly for supporting the book. The website contains over eight hours of high-definition videos of me instructing and performing each of the lessons, making understanding and performing each lesson a breeze. Just go to **www.pianoinstruction.com** and register for the free videos.

A Professional Way of Playing Chords

This book will teach you how to use shells and patterns in the left hand, using chord parts including the root, 5th, 7th, and 10th to provide the bass sound, tempo, and rhythm for a tune. In the right hand, you will learn how to apply the 3rd of the chord for harmonies, effectively spreading the chord across both hands in a very professional manner.

Understanding Improvisation

The topic of diatonic patterns with improvisation is an initial introduction into freeform improvisation that allows you to sit at the piano and play, creating the music as you go. You will quickly be creating enjoyable music while training your hands to move freely around the keyboard.

Blues Playing

The book also introduces the blues. Six blues tunes that I have written are included. With each tune, I show you how to play the tune using our shell techniques. Then I show you how to apply blues improvisation using the C blues scale in your right hand and shells to the 5th and patterns in your left hand. It is a fun improvisational style of playing.

Tunes at Four Levels

All the weeks are accompanied by tunes. These tunes are presented at four different levels: Tune with Shells, Tune with Shells to the 5th, Tune with Patterns, and Tune with 3rds on Compression. Start with shells in Week 1, and tackle the other levels as you move through the book. These tunes prepare you to choose your own favorites, and we encourage you to get some lead sheets of your favorite tunes and work on them in conjunction with the rest of the lessons. You can never have too many fake books; they supply ready access to a multitude of popular favorites.

   Most of all, have some fun, learn some skills. Use them for the rest of your life. Play.

Getting Started

By now, you should know that each week covers an aspect of shells, patterns, the 3rd, stride, diatonic improvisation, blues, and applying these to tunes. Also, you should know that you must have some piano background to start this book.

For My Beginner's Book Students

If your background includes our beginner's book, *Learn to Play Piano in Six Weeks or Less*, you should be ready to start off with Week 1.

For Chord-Playing Students

If your background is other chord-based techniques, Week 1 is a good starting point, but you might also go to Appendices A and B to take a look at "What is a Shell?" and "How to Find the 5th" to understand the professional chord technique that we use in the book.

For Students with a Classical Background

If your background is a classical bass clef/treble clef reading method, then you surely want to look at "What is a Shell?" in Appendix A and "How to Find the 5th" in Appendix B.

Important Skills in Our Appendix

The appendix also includes lessons on counting and scales. These are important skills, and you may need to brush up on them. As with all of the lessons in the book, the appendix lessons are supported by online videos.

Once you get through these startup steps, begin with Week 1. Go through the week, trying to do all 6 lessons every day you sit down at the piano, 5 or 10 minutes for each lesson. Optionally, refer to the videos to see and hear how I play the lesson. When you feel comfortable with the lessons, move on to Week 2.

Week 1

Week 1 sets up the entire flow of the lessons of the book, and for this reason it is an important week of lessons. Week 1 can also be the most difficult week of the book, depending on your background. Take it easy, in small steps, and by the end of the week you will be on your way.

The Six Topics

The topics I present are Shells, The 3rd, Patterns, Stride, Diatonic Improvisation, and Playing the Blues; plus you get six tunes included at the end of the book, each played at 4 different levels. Week 1 will get you started with a full explanation of each of these topics, as well as your first lesson in each of them. As mentioned in the introduction, try to spend a little time on each of the topics every time you sit down to practice.

How to Practice

Break It Down: When you first start on an exercise, or a tune, break it down into levels. Start with the left hand only, then the right hand only. Simplify what you do in the left or the right hand. As you become comfortable with the simplified levels, move your way up to more challenging techniques. You may not get there in the first day, so increase the challenge every day you practice.

Levels: I suggest varying levels of difficulty throughout the lessons. Start at Level 1 and move to the higher levels as you become comfortable.

Fragmenting: Fragmenting is a technique I often talk about in my videos. With fragmenting, you break down the exercise into small parts; one measure, or two measures, or one line at a time. By going over this small piece until you get it right, you will absorb the material faster.

The 3 Rule: When fragmenting a part of the music, I suggest using my 3 Rule to test your comfort with the fragment. Play it through 3 times with no mistakes and you are ready to move on. It is best to keep content down to small chunks. The student that plays straight through from the beginning to the end will often not progress as quickly as those who take the time to fragment and break down the lesson material.

What You Need to Know to Start

I realize that this book will be used by people of different playing backgrounds. These differences will be greatest during the first week of the book. For that reason, I have put a few lessons in the Appendix that help to get everyone on the same page; aids to understanding my terminology and some of the base concepts.

The Root, the 5th, and the 7th: The key concept to understand is in your left hand: taking a chord and breaking it down to a 2-note shell consisting of the root and the 7th. That is followed by adding in the 5th. There is a very simple technique for finding the root, the 7th, and the 5th for all chords, and I show that technique in Appendix A and Appendix B.

Beginner's Book Owners: Those of you who have my original *Learn to Play Piano in Six Weeks or Less* book will remember these Appendix lessons. You may want to look at them again to refresh your memory.

Chord Players: Those of you who have chord-playing knowledge can use the Appendix A and B lessons to learn how I break chords into the shell followed by the 5th rather than playing triads. Some practice will be needed to be comfortable with finding the shell and the 5th for all chord types. This is important to your success with the book.

Bass Clef–Treble Clef Readers: Those of you who are traditional bass clef–treble clef readers will have to spend a little more time with the shells and the 5th. But I have found that your left-hand reading skills mean you are very comfortable with your left hand, and that in turn simplifies the task. The Appendix A and B lessons will give you everything you need.

This first week is the toughest of all, but don't get discouraged. In this week we are building the foundation of your playing skills. In the following weeks it becomes easier because we only need to incrementally build on your techniques. Those of you new to my methods may need to take a little more than a week to get comfortable with the first week of the book.

Week 1
What You Will Learn in Week 1

Shell to the 5th: Shell to the 5th is a key technique used in your left hand to frame the chord and apply timing and rhythm. It is one of the top five techniques taught in the book, and you will use it always in your playing.

3rd & ♭3rd: The 3rd is possibly the most important chord tone to understand. It defines a chord as a major or minor chord. Using the 3rd is a top five technique.

Major7 3-Note Patterns: 1–5–octave and 1–5–7 left hand patterns are introduced for major7 chords. They are exercised with the 3rd in your right hand, another top five technique.

Diatonic 3-Note Patterns: Learn the seven diatonic patterns, and how to do simple improvisation using key note releases in your right hand.

Blues Tune Example: Play one of my blues tunes using Shell to the 5th. Learn the C blues scale and apply it in improvisation against the chords of the tune.

Tunes: Introduction to one of the six tunes supplied with the book. Description of how to play the tune using all the techniques taught in the book. The complete set of tunes with instructions on how to apply my techniques is included after the lessons of week 6, each presented in the same format shown here. Visit this area to play some tunes at any time in the book. Also supply your own favorite tunes and apply my techniques.

Shells
What You Will Learn About Shells
We start the shell lessons with concentrating on your left hand and becoming facile with the root, 5th, and 7th. In later weeks, I also cover how to apply the 3rd and the ♭3rd in the right hand. By the end of the book, you will be comfortable with spreading pieces of the chord across both hands, a very professional technique.

What Do You Need to Know Before Starting This Lesson?
As mentioned in the introduction, you need to know the root, 5th, and 7th. Appendix A and Appendix B supply exercises and videos to bring you up to speed.

The Video: *Week 1: 5ths and Shells*

5ths & Shells
The first week on shells gets you going with applying 5ths to the shell, for both tonal and rhythmic enhancement. This is the first very important step in getting movement and rhythm in your left hand. You will use this forever in your playing. This is one of my top five skills.

First and foremost, you should be comfortable with finding the 5th for all chords. In short, the 5th is either a white-key root to a white-key 5th spanning 5 white keys, or a black-key root to a black-key 5th spanning 4 black keys, or the special case of A♯, B♭, or B. If you have problems, you can refer to Appendix B, where we have some exercises for finding the 5th. The illustration below may help.

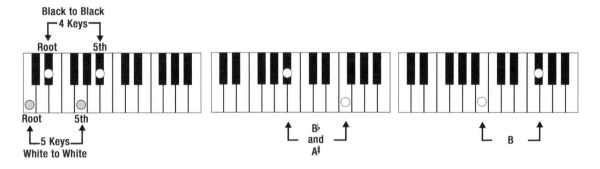

The technique of shell to the 5th is accomplished by playing the shell on beat 1 for 2 beats, followed by the 5th on beat 3 for 2 beats. Below is an illustration of the shell and 5th for Cmaj7 played with the pinky (5), index finger (2), and thumb (1), as well as 2 bars showing how you would play shell to the 5th including pedaling.

This is the most difficult lesson in Week 1, as well as one of the most important techniques in the book. You should watch the video to hear and view this important technique.

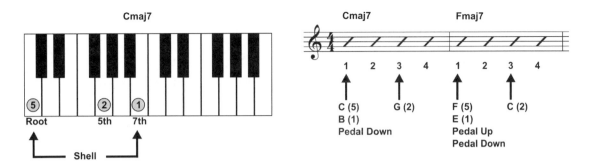

The best way to attack this piece (5ths & Shells worksheet, page 7), and actually the best way to attack all pieces, is to break it down into levels and work through the levels until you are comfortable.

Level 1: Start working on the first line of the music shown below, just playing the melody in the right hand alone.

Level 2: Go through the first line again (shown below), playing the root of the shell in the left hand along with the melody in the right.

Levels 3 & 4: Then try the shells in the left hand alone shown below, followed by shells and the melody.

Level 5: Then play the shells to the 5th in the left hand alone.

Level 6: Finally, play the shell to the 5th in the left hand along with the melody in the right. When you are comfortable with the first line, move on to the next line in the worksheet. Continue until you complete the piece.

Pedaling

Pedaling is important in this technique. Refer to the graphic on the following page. Put down the sustain pedal at the start of the first chord. Let it up and put it down again at the next chord. When pedaling, it is an opposite effect. The pedal comes up when the next chord goes down, then it goes immediately back down again. Pedaling has two effects; letting it up shuts off the sound being held from the previous chord, and putting it down holds the new sound for the new chord. Just remember that throughout the piece, the first thing you do as you play a chord is to let the pedal up to shut off the previous chord, then follow with immediately putting it down to sustain the new chord.

Practice this, playing the shells in the left hand only. Shell down, pedal up then down. You can apply this while playing the piece, or, if need be, break it down and first try it while playing the shell to the 5th in the left hand only. The graphic below illustrates the pedal timing.

The pedal gives you an opportunity to position your left hand for the next chord. After playing the 5th on beat 3, you have the rest of beat 3 and beat 4 to freely move your left hand; the pedal is sustaining the tones. With practice, you should be able to have your left hand positioned by beat 4.

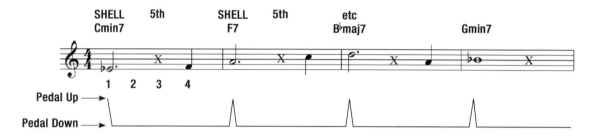

Chord Isolation

A great simplification level is chord isolation, where you play the shell or shell to the 5th in the left hand and only the first note of the melody under the chord in the right hand. Here is an example of the first line played as chord isolation.

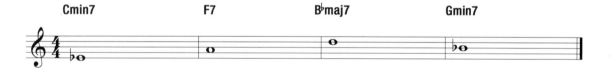

By breaking your lesson down and becoming comfortable with your lesson a chunk at a time, you make it easier to learn the lesson.

Have some fun with this lesson. It gives you an important skill that will help you provide movement and timing to your playing. You will use this for the rest of your life.

5th & Shells Worksheet
2516 Application

Level 1: Right Hand melody only.

Level 2: Root of chord in Left Hand, melody in Right Hand.

Levels 3 & 4: Shells only in the Left, then add melody in the Right.

Level 5: Shell to 5th only in the Left.

Level 6: Shell to 5th in the Left, melody in the Right.

Pedal in all Levels.

5ths & Shells Worksheet

3rds

What You Will Learn

The 3rd is a very important note. It tells you whether a chord is a major chord or a minor chord. It is the chord tone that you will later move into your right hand, to start the spread of the chord across both your hands. You will learn to find all the 3rds in 4 chord types.

The Video: *Week 1: 3rds Memorization*

Finding the 3rd

Take a look at the C Major scale and see where the 3rd is found.

The 3rd is found in these chord types:

Major   maj7   aug7   maj6

Different publishers will use different "short-hand" notations for the chords (e.g., maj7 or M7). See page 109 for a full list of notations for all chords.

In this lesson, you are going to have to memorize the third in all keys. There are only 12 of them, so it's not that hard.

Level 1

We will start by looking at the 3rd interval shape, looking at the root and the 3rd as shown below.

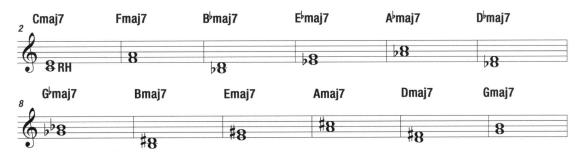

Play through the two lines above, both notes in the right hand. After going through these lines a few times, play through the master progression shown below, playing the root and the 3rd in your right hand. In this case, you will have to figure out the third yourself. Try not to refer to the lines above for assistance.

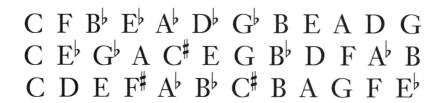

Master Progression

Level 2

Once you have this going well, you should do the same 2 steps spreading the 2 notes further apart to the 10th interval. The 10th is just the 3rd, an octave higher. An example of the 10th interval is shown below. Play it, and then go through the master progression again, playing the root and the 10th.

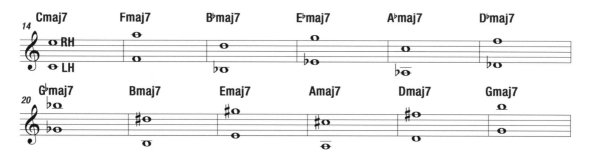

Level 3: Application

The next step is to start playing the root in your left hand and the 3rd in your right hand. You can spread the left and right hands by as many octaves as you like. You can move up to playing maj7 chords in your left hand and the 3rd in your right hand. Play a shell or shell to the 5th. The easiest way is to play the chord on beat 1 and the 3rd on beat 4. A little more difficult is to play them all on beat 1.

Final Notes:

- The 3rd determines whether a chord is major or minor. It is an important note.
- Work until you can find the 3rd easily.
- Try to remember the 3rd by itself, not the 3rd interval shape.
- Remember to pedal; it's good practice.

3rds Memorization Worksheet

The 3rd of the chord is derived from the Major Scale.

Level 1: Play 3rd Interval **Shape** through all keys—try not to look at the written ones above for the answer.

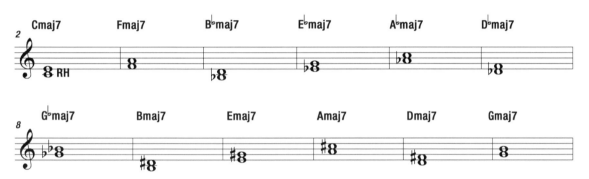

Level 2: Play 10th Interval **Shape** through all keys with **wide** application.

10th Interval Shape: This wide interval really helps learn the 3rd.

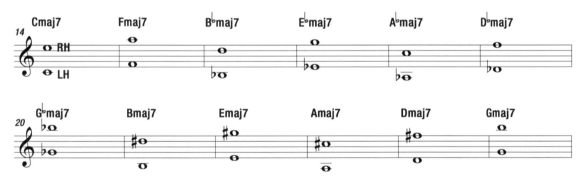

C F B♭ E♭ A♭ D♭ G♭ B E A D G

C E♭ G♭ A C♯ E G B♭ D F A♭ B

C D E F♯ A♭ B♭ C♯ B A G F E♭

Master Progression

Level 3 Application: Left hand plays the Shell or Shell to 5th while the Right Hand is playing the 3rd of each chord.

      *You may also play Patterns built on the Shell. 157
      *Right Hand may be applied on the beat or on beat 4.

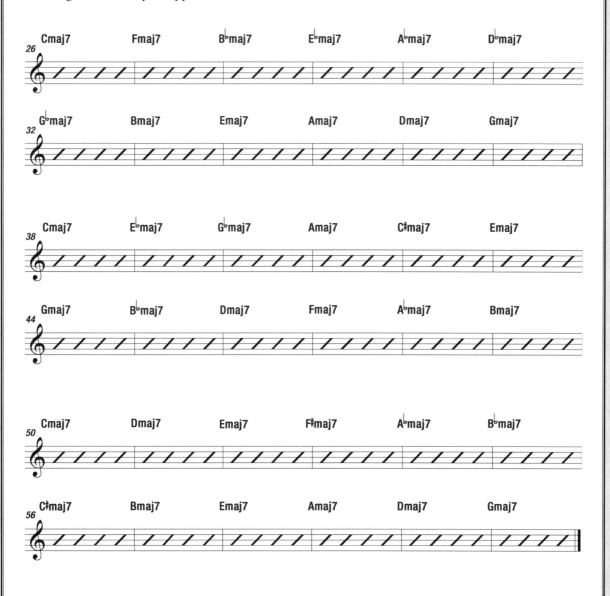

♭3rds: Finding the ♭3rd
What You will Learn

The ♭3rd is a very important note. It makes the chord a minor chord. The ♭3rd is just a half step below the 3rd, as shown below. You will learn to find all the ♭3rds in 5 different chord types.

The Video: *Week 1: ♭3rds Memorization*

Finding the ♭3rd

The ♭3rd is found in these chord types:

Minor	min7	min7♭5	dim7	min6

Different publishers will use different "short-hand" notations for the chords (e.g., maj7 or M7). See page 109 for a full list of notations for all chords.

Level 1

We will start by looking at the ♭3rd interval shape, looking at the root and the ♭3rd as shown below.

Play through the 2 lines above, both notes in the right hand. After going through these lines a few times, play through the Master Progression shown below, playing the root and the ♭3rd in your right hand. In this case, you will have to figure out the ♭3rd yourself. Try not to refer to the lines above for assistance.

Master Progression

Level 2

Once you have this going well, you should move up to the ♭10th interval. The ♭10th is just the ♭3rd, an octave higher. Play the 2 lines below, playing the root in your left hand and the ♭10th in your right hand. You could even play the right hand a few octaves higher.

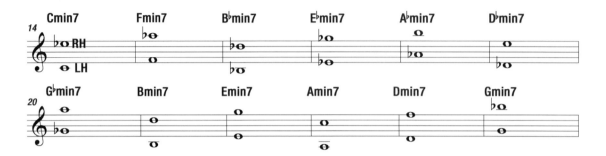

When comfortable with these two lines, move on to playing through the master progression; play the root in your left hand and the ♭10th in your right hand. You need to find the ♭10th on the fly without referring to the written sheets of music or the ♭10th interval.

Level 3 Application

The next step is to go through the master progression on the second page of the worksheet. This time, move up to playing min7 chords in your left hand and the ♭3rd in your right hand. Play a shell or shell to the 5th in your left hand. The easiest way is to play the chord on beat 1 (and beat 3) and the ♭3rd on beat 4. A little more difficult is to play them all on beat 1.

Final Notes:

- Make sure you know the ♭3rds before starting.
- Work until you can find the ♭3rd easily.
- Try to remember the ♭3rds by themselves, not the ♭3rd interval shape.
- The ♭3rd does not have to be a black note.
- Remember to pedal; it's good practice.

♭3rds Memorization Worksheet

Level 1: Play ♭3rd Interval **Shape** through all keys—try not to look at the written ones above for the answer.

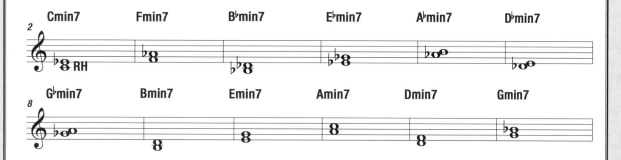

Level 2: Play ♭10th Interval **Shape** through all keys with **wide** application.

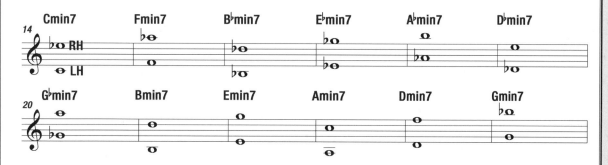

C F B♭ E♭ A♭ D♭ G♭ B E A D G

C E♭ G♭ A C# E G B D F A♭ B

C D E F# A♭ B♭ C# B A G F E♭

Master Progression

Level 3 Application: Left hand plays the Shell or (Shell to 5th), while the Right Hand is playing the ♭3rd of each chord.

    *You may also play Patterns built on the Shell. 157
    *Right Hand may be applied on the beat or on beat 4.

Important: Chord Types that the ♭3rd work on

Minor	Min7	Min7♭5	Min6	Dim7
1 ♭3 5	1 ♭3 5 ♭7	1 ♭3 ♭5 ♭7	1 ♭3 5 6	1 ♭3 ♭5 ♭♭7

Patterns

What You Will Learn

The patterns are a very important chord-playing skill that will establish time and motion in your playing. Patterns are a left-hand technique that can be a standalone style or can be used in conjunction with shells and shell to the 5th. By the end of this book, you should be comfortable with patterns for all chord types in all keys. You will be able to combine these patterns with the techniques you learned in the other topics, applying them to every piece you play. You will see that patterns are a very nice way to present chords, one tone at a time. This week will teach you the Major 7th base patterns of root–5–octave and root–5–7.

What Do You Need to Start This Lesson?

Just as in the shells lessons, you need to know the root (or the 1), the 5th, and the 7th. Appendix A and Appendix B supply exercises and videos to bring you up to speed.

The Video: *Week 1: Base Patterns Octave Maj7*

Major 7th Base Patterns

Patterns can be very important parts of your playing, as they can effectively outline the chord. In this first week, we will be setting up two patterns for the Major 7th chords, the 1–5–octave, and the 1–5–7. You will be playing the patterns in your left hand, a melody in your right hand, and, as a final step, playing the 3rd in your right hand. Adding the 3rd in the right hand starts the training of playing all 4 tones of the chord.

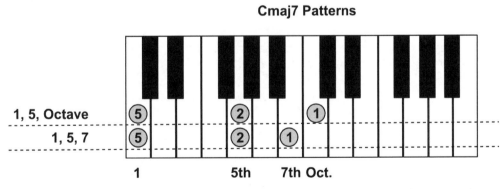

Cmaj7 Patterns

Patterns played pinky(5), index finger (2) and thumb (1)
or
pinky(5), middle finger (3), and thumb (1)

In this lesson, I want you to cycle through all the 12 Major 7th chords. The easiest way to cycle is to use one of the lines of the Master Progression shown on the right, Cmaj7 followed by Fmaj7 etc. You will find that this lesson not only gets you used to the patterns, but also gives you lots of practice finding the 3rd.

$$C \quad F \quad B^\flat \quad E^\flat \quad A^\flat \quad D^\flat \quad G^\flat \quad B \quad E \quad A \quad D \quad G$$

$$C \quad E^\flat \quad G^\flat \quad A \quad C^\sharp \quad E \quad G \quad B^\flat \quad D \quad F \quad A^\flat \quad B$$

$$C \quad D \quad E \quad F^\sharp \quad A^\flat \quad B^\flat \quad C^\sharp \quad B \quad A \quad G \quad F \quad E^\flat$$

Master Progression

Level 1: Left Hand Only

Play the 1–5–octave pattern in your left hand. Cycle through the first line of the master progression, your left hand playing the 1, the 5th, and the octave on beats 1, 2, and 3 respectively. Play the 1 with your pinkie, the 5th with your index finger (or middle finger), and the octave with your thumb. When you are comfortable with this pattern, cycle through the master progression, playing the 1–5–7 pattern in your left hand.

Pedaling

In these exercises you should get into the practice of using the sustain pedal to give a nice full tone. Press the pedal down as you start the pattern in the first bar. At bar 2 and all the following bars, let the pedal up as you start the pattern, and then place it back down again. I call this the opposite effect. Pedal up as the first note of the pattern goes down. Then the pedal goes back down. The graphic below illustrates the pedal timing.

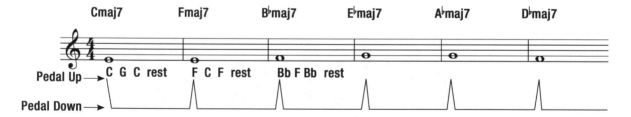

Level 2: Left and Right Hands

Play one of the patterns in your left hand, either 1–5–octave or 1–5–7. In your right hand play the whole note melody as written in the Base Patterns Worksheet (page 20). Cycle through the three master progression melodies on the worksheet. An example is below.

Level 3: Find your own 3rds

Play one of the patterns in your left hand on beats 1, 2, and 3, and the quarter note 3rd on beat 4 in your right hand. The 3rd is a very important note that we will be moving into your right hand throughout the weeks. Play through the master progression, playing the pattern in your left hand followed by the 3rd in your right hand.

Final Notes:

- Fragment where necessary. Play a line or a bar or two repeating until you are comfortable.
- Don't rush; keep it slow and smooth.
- Pedal to get a full tone from the individual notes of the pattern.
- Keep your left hand near your right hand; don't get too low. Sometimes you have two choices where you might want to play your left hand.
- This lesson gives a good start on learning how to place the 3rd in your right hand.

Base Patterns Worksheet
1 5 Octave–1 5 7
(Major 7)–Octave Range

Octave Range: Here we look at the first 2 Base Patterns that will be framed in the Left Hand within the Octave range. It is important to master these in all 12 keys.

Left Hand												
1 5 Octave	C	F	B♭	E♭	A♭	D	G♭	B	E	A	D	G
1 5 7	C	E♭	G♭	A	C♯	E	G	B♭	D	F	A♭	B
	C	D	E	F♯	G♯	B♭	C♯	B	A	G	F	E♭

Master Progression

Level 1: Left Hand Only

Left Hand Pattern by itself through all keys. (Vary order through Master Progression.)

Level 2: Left and Right Hands

Apply both Left Hand Octave Range Patterns through the 3 progressions against the melody.

Cycle 5 Progression

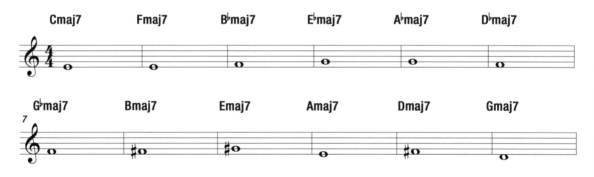

Diminished Progression

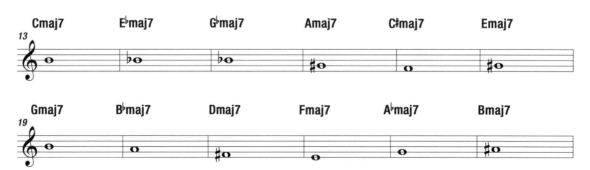

Whole Tone Progression

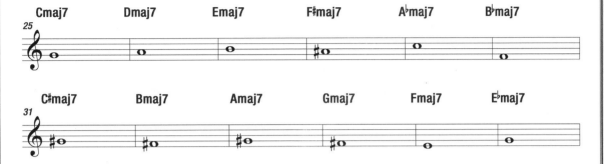

Level 3: Find your own 3rds
Left Hand–Choose Pattern
Right Hand–Play 3rd of chord on beat 4

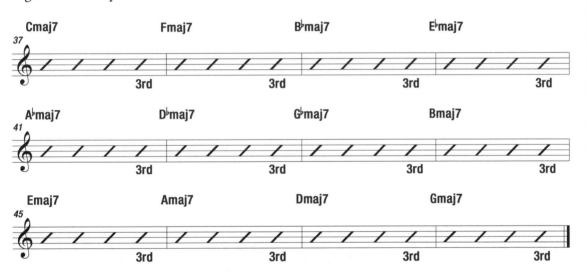

The 3rd will be a very important note in our playing and while learning the Left Hand. I find it very helpful to be practicing the 3rd into the Right Hand through all keys.

Diatonic Improvisation
What You Will Learn

Diatonic means "all notes in the same key," and I have designed our diatonic improvisation track to use the key of C. This means that all white notes, and white notes only, are available for improvisation. I have created 3-note patterns to use, one for each of the seven notes in the C scale. These patterns also contain only white notes. This week you will learn all 7 diatonic patterns and how to improvise with them.

The Video: *Week1: Key Note Release with single notes and textures*

Improvisation Made Easy

The diatonic improvisation lessons are simplified by using only 7 patterns and only white notes. This limited set allows you to focus on improvisation skills, choosing notes and chords from a simplified group. Later in this book, I will show you how to merge the diatonics with all our other techniques, giving you a platform for some improvisational exploration on your own.

No Music Sheet: The lessons in this track won't be focused on a sheet of music as the base of your playing. Instead, they will be focused on choosing your own chords for your left hand and your own right-hand notes, and being comfortable making choices that allow your hands to improvise together. Simplifying your choices lets you concentrate more on the interplay between your two hands, making you comfortable improvising your own pieces in this limited space. It is the perfect way to become acquainted with the improvisational world of playing.

Diatonic 3-note patterns: The image below shows the seven patterns. Each pattern contains 3 notes that you should play in your left hand, one note per beat on the first 3 beats of the measure. The diatonic-patterns illustration also points out a right-hand key note and a void note for each pattern.

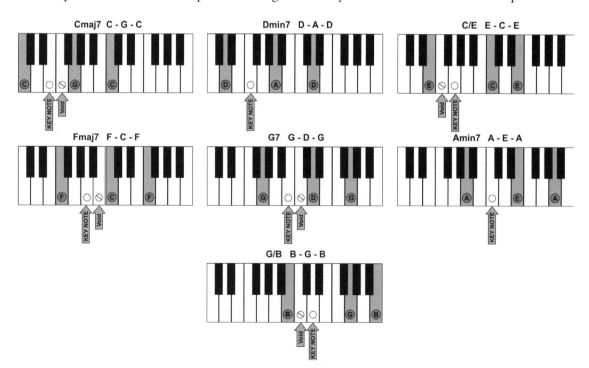

Key Note Release with 3-Note Patterns

In this lesson, the left hand plays the 7 diatonic 3-note patterns while the right hand plays a dotted half note followed by a quarter note releasing to the dotted half note of the next measure. The dotted half note is always the key note of the 3-note pattern for that bar.

Level 1

Run through all the 3-note patterns and their key notes, playing the 3-note pattern in the left hand while playing whole-note key notes in the right hand. The example below gets you started.

Remember to pedal. As you start a pattern, pedal up, then immediately back down. After playing the pattern on beats one, two, and three, you will have beat four to lift your left hand and position it for the next pattern; the pedal will be holding your pattern tones. The graphic below illustrates the pedal timing.

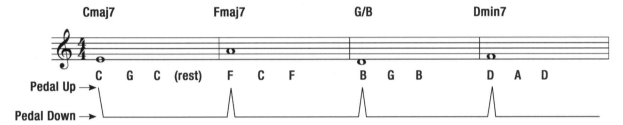

Once you are comfortable with each 3-note pattern and its key note, proceed to level 2.

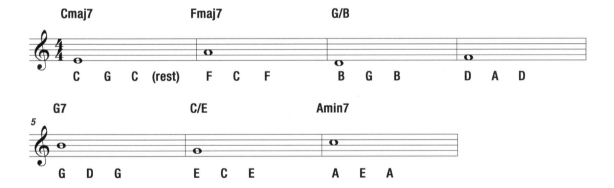

Level 2

Go through all the 3-note patterns using a dotted half note to quarter note in your right hand, releasing to the key notes of each of the other patterns. For each of these releases, choose a note that is one note higher or lower than the key note that is the target of your release. The example below does this for Cmaj7 to all the other patterns. When you are done with the example, continue on for Dmin7 to all other patterns, and then C/E, etc.

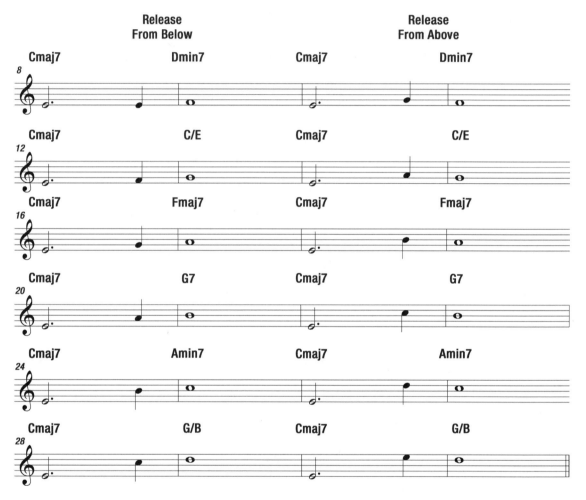

Continue this exercise for Dmin7, C/E, Fmaj7, G7, Amin7, G/B.

Level 3

Choose your own releases. Start with any 3-note pattern and release to any other 3-note pattern that you choose. Keep going; you could do this all afternoon. It is fun and musical, and you will find many pleasing combinations. Start with the example below, and then continue on your own.

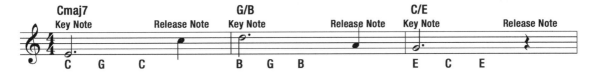

Level 4

This level expands upon Level 3 in that you play textures for the key note. A texture is a 2-note pair. Create your texture by playing a second note below the key note, holding them both for the 3 beats. The texture note can be just below the key note, or it could be a separation of 4 or 5 notes. I call these narrow and wide textures. Play around with what sounds good. Sometimes you might get an odd-sounding pair, and that is probably because you hit upon a void note in your texture. Don't worry, I will cover what to do with those later.

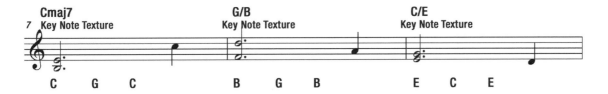

Level 5

This level expands on Level 4 by adding a texture to the release note as well as the key note. This is a high level and it sounds great, but it is a challenge. It will be very rewarding when you become comfortable with it.

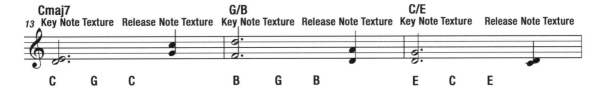

Freeform

Although I teach specific key notes, once you are comfortable you may create your own spontaneous improvisation using a variety of note selections; you will be free to choose notes other than key notes. Because this topic is presented in the key of C, all white notes will work—although you will notice that the void notes don't work well unless immediately resolved to another note.

Key Note Release Worksheet
Single Notes & Textures

Release: The "release" can be up or down and can move any distance from the very next note to leaping to a larger interval.

The Next Chord: This Released Tone will help us identify the next Chord to be played. So, as you look at the Release Tone, look at the very next note higher or lower. That is the New Key Note for the next 3-Note Pattern to be played. The options become very vast here as you have full control of choosing the released tone.

The Key Note will be played for 3 beats and the Release Note is on beat 4.

Level 1: Be able to play all Key Notes comfortably for each of the 7 Diatonic 3-Note Patterns.

Level 2: Take each of the 3-Note Patterns and explore Releasing to each white note that can be chosen. Creating a 2-pattern loop example below.

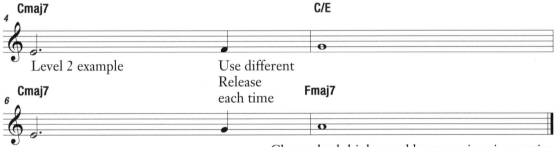

Level 2 example

Use different Release each time

Choose both higher and lower options in practice.

Level 3: Fully function exploring as many released tones as you can. Identify next chord quickly!

Level 4: Textures: You may play any white note below the Key Note, creating 2-Note texture.

Level 5: Textures: You can create textures on both the Key Note and Release Note, always creating the texture with a white note below that focuses tone.

Blues Tunes
What You Will Learn

Each week you will learn how to apply the techniques you are learning to some of my original blues tunes. This week you play a tune using our shell to the 5th technique, and we will explore basic blues scale improvisation. The C blues scale is an easy-to-use tool that will help you rapidly and smoothly play notes that will work over the chords. You will see how the blues is a combination of what you are learning with a few specialized items like the blues scale to get the particular blues sound.

The Video: *Week1: Table Rock Levels up to 3rd*

Table Rock

Each of these blues tunes is a piece that I wrote and I include in my professional gigs all the time. Table Rock is a nice simple piece. In this first blues tune, I want you to focus on getting your left hand working with options against the tune. You will also be introduced to the C blues scale. The score is shown on the following page.

Level 1: Bass Notes

Start by playing the basic tune, using only the root of the chord as bass notes in the left hand. Feel free to play these notes very low; it sounds great. Play the tune in the right hand.

Level 2: Shell to the 5th

Once you become comfortable with the tune, move up to shell to the 5th in the left hand. In this tune, it will be on beats 1 and 2, and again on beats 3 and 4. Or, you can try playing shells or even pulsing a shell in the left hand, one pulse every beat.

Level 3: The C Blues Scale

Now, take a look at the C blues scale on the worksheet. You can use this scale throughout all eight bars of this tune. Note the fingering: it is primarily 1, 3, 1, 3, 1, 3 or thumb, middle finger, thumb, middle finger. Try running this scale up and down the keyboard; don't stop at just one octave, go all the way. You can throw in a 5 (pinky) when you want to turn around and go back down the keyboard, or just turn on the 1 or 3. Get comfortable with the scale by using lots of turns in the scale itself; also try playing the scale starting at different places within the scale.

C blues scale eighth notes: For the first application of the blues scale, use eighth notes in the right hand, four notes per chord. Just play the scale up and down the keyboard as you play the shells to the 5th in your left hand.

C blues scale rock: An even easier way to get started with the blues scale is to just rock, playing the same 1, 3 pair over and over. Mix the rock with some traveling up and down.

C blues scale repeat: Even simpler is just to repeat the same note for a measure or a chord. At the beginning, if you have problems, just fragment a couple of measures at a time. Go slow, start with an easy concept, and make sure you have a solid shell to the 5th going in the left-hand.

Table Rock

Level 1: Bass Notes and Tune

Level 2: Shell to 5th and Tune

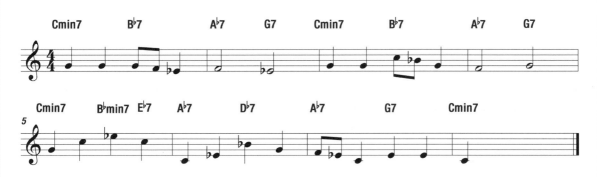

Level 3: C Blues Scale

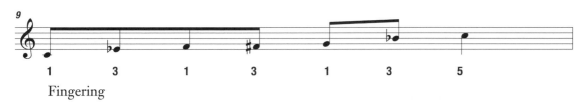

Fingering

Improvisation

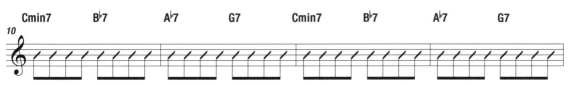

1/8 notes: Here we use the C Blues Scale, playing 4 notes per chord for this top line.

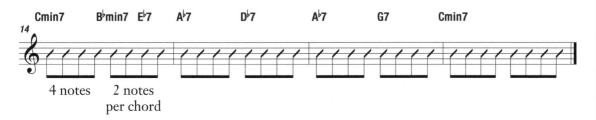

4 notes   2 notes
           per chord

Important: The C Blues Scale notes will work for the entire 8 bars. Once you are comfortable with the Tune, you can then explore the improvisational ideas using the C Blues Scale notes against the Left Hand Chords. Keep tempo slow.

Tunes
What You Will Learn

Each week, I would like you to work on a tune to apply the techniques that you have learned during the week. Six tunes are presented following week 6 of the book (pages 128–151). Each of these tunes is played in four different styles: Shell and Melody, Shell to the 5th, Base Patterns, and 3rds on Compression.

The tunes presented are *Indian Summer*, *After You've Gone*, *My Wild Irish Rose*, *Back Home in Indiana*, *Happy Birthday*, and *Shenandoah*. You can play any one of these tunes any time; they each have notes on how to play them with the variety of styles taught in this book. For a little continuity, you can play then in the order presented.

The Video: *Indian Summer with Shells and Melody*
The Video: *Indian Summer with Shells to the 5th and Melody*
The Video: *Indian Summer with Base Patterns applied*
The Video: *Indian Summer with 3rds on Compression*

Your Own Tunes

You should also try this out on your own favorite tunes. It's a great learning method, and, after all, that's what you eventually want to do. Why not start now? It's fun, it's a challenge, and often it is the inspiration you need to keep going.

Start out playing the tunes with Shells and Melody, and move up to the other more difficult styles as you progress through the book.

Indian Summer
Shell in the Left Hand

The *Indian Summer* score is found on page 33. The shell is an important technique; it is a professional technique that you need to get down solidly. It is the foundation for the upcoming styles of shell to the 5th, patterns, and 3rds on compression, even in the future techniques of bounce, pulse, and stride. Make sure you get comfortable with it.

To start, notice the key signature of the key of G where every F is sharp. You will notice that throughout the tune, as in bar 2, there are quarter-note triplets. What is a triplet? It is 3 notes that need to be played in the time of two beats. So a quarter-note triplet is three notes that need to be played in the two beats allotted to two quarter notes. You need to play all three notes of the triplet in two beats. They are tough to count. I count them **1+e2+e** with the notes evenly spaced on 1, the e of 1, and the + of 2. It's more of a feeling kind of thing, rather than an out-and-out counting. Play through the tune, watch for the triplets (listen to the video), and enjoy.

Shell to the 5th

Shell to the 5th is a great way to keep time and set a rhythm. It's a mainstay of your playing. As you play the tune, the shell and the 5th fall on the first and third beat respectively. When you run across two chords in a bar, as in bar 2, play just the shell.

You will come across a flat 5th in bars 6, 9, and 22, where you run across dim7 and min7♭5 chords. You may want to pencil this in on the piece so you remember when you get there. Just move the 5th 1 step down to the ♭5th in these cases.

Left-Hand Placement

Sometimes you will have a choice of where to play the left hand. I like to keep the left hand close to the right as the tune moves up and down the keyboard, but sometimes you run into an overlap between the two and you might want to lower the left hand an octave. It's a personal preference, but either choice is correct.

Pedaling

Pedaling becomes more important with shell to the 5th. You don't want to have to hold the 5th too long, because you need some time to set up for the next chord. If you pedal correctly, you have all of beat 4 to set up for the next chord. Pedaling has two opposite effects: letting it up shuts off the sound being held, and putting it down holds the new sound. You should depress the sustain pedal at the start of a chord, and release and depress the pedal at the start of the next chord. This way, the 5th and the chord will continue to ring as you move your left hand to the next chord. The graphic below illustrates the pedal timing.

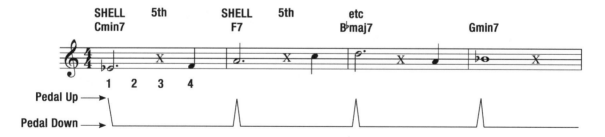

Chord Isolation

Chord isolation is a great way to get started on a tune or to take a break for a couple of bars. Chord isolation is playing the note below the chord for the entire measure, ignoring the rest of the melody. It allows you to concentrate on your left hand.

Importantly, you should use this tune as a reference, a way to get started presenting these styles. You should also apply these styles to some of your own favorite tunes. With each tune, start at the lowest level and work up. Go through the progression of left hand only, right hand only, root and melody, shell and melody, shell to the 5th, patterns, and 3rds on compression. All along the way, throw in chord isolation when you need it. Fragment as well to get comfortable.

Base Patterns

I have four base patterns that you will be learning to use on your tunes.

    1, 5, octave   1, 5, 7   1, 5, 10   1, 7, 10

Start off the first few weeks using 1, 5, octave or 1, 5, 7. In week 2, you will have learned enough about the 3rd (and the 10th, which is an octave above the 3rd) that you can start using 1, 5, 10 and 1, 7, 10 for patterns if you feel you are ready.

When you have two chords to a measure in your tune, as in bar 2, modify the pattern to a 2-note pattern like 1–5 or 1–octave or 1–7. Once you know the 10ths, you can use 1–10 as a 2-note pattern. You could even do shell to the 5th on beats 1 and 2 if you want. If the 5th is in your pattern, watch out for the ♭5ths in bars 6, 9, and 22.

Remember chord isolation if this gets too difficult.

3rds on Compression

Save this style for weeks 3 through 6. I cover it in depth during week 2 and week 3.

Play through the tune using shells to the 5th in the left hand. In the right hand add the 3rd below the melody note as you are compressing the root of the chord in your left hand. In the case where the melody note is the third, as in bars 1 and 3, you don't add an additional note. Optionally, you could add a 3rd an octave below the 3rd in the melody. Either choice is correct.

In a similar manner, when the melody note and the 3rd are right next to each other, you can choose to play the third an octave lower if you can reach it.

If the melody note doesn't occur at chord compression, as in bars 2, 4, 8, 12, and others, you have options as well. You could add the 3rd in with the chord compression, or you could delay the 3rd to occur at the same time as the melody note.

Let's review what you have learned this week.

Indian Summer

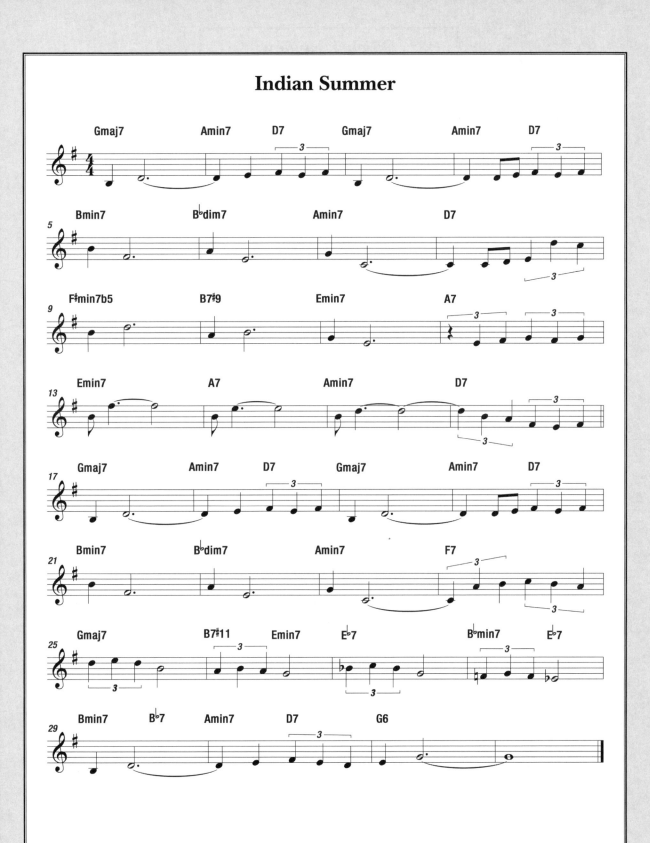

Week 1 Review

Shells

- Are you comfortable with the shell of all chords?
- Can you find the 5th for all chords?
- Can you play the shell to the 5th for all chords?
- Are you comfortable with pedaling?

Patterns

- Can you play the exercise sheet using a root, 5, octave pattern?
- Can you play the exercise sheet using a root, 5, 7 pattern?

3rds

- Can you find the 3rds and ♭3rds for all 12 keys?
- Can you find the 10th and flat 10th for all 12 keys?
- Do you know what chord types contain the 3rd?
- Do you know what chord types contain the ♭3rd?

Diatonic Improvisation

- Can you play all 7 diatonic 3-note patterns?
- Can you play the key notes in the right hand with the patterns?
- Can you play a key note release in the right hand along with a pattern?
- Can you play a continuous stream of patterns and releases?
- Can you add a texture to the key note?
- Can you add a texture to the release note?

Blues

- Can you play the blues tune using the left-hand options of shell, shell to the 5th, and pulse?
- Can you rock two notes in the C blues scale?
- Can you repeat a note continuously in the C blues scale?
- Can you play the C blues scale up and down the keyboard?
- Can you substitute the C blues scale for the melody of the tune?

Tunes

- Can you play the tune using shells?
- Can you play the tune using shell to the 5th?
- Can you play the tune using patterns?

Remember that Week 1 is the hardest week in the book, and it is the foundation of everything to come. If you need to spend some extra days on this week, take the extra time to become comfortable.

Week 2

Skills You Will Learn in Week 2

The 5th in the left hand 1–5–7 3-note pattern: Learn to play 3-note patterns by adding the 5th to the shell and creating the 1–5–7 3-note pattern. Learn how the 5th changes with the min7♭5, dim7, and aug7 chords. Another top five skill.

The 3rd on Compression: You will learn how to play the 3rd on compression with the shell in your right hand, using a melody consisting of whole notes. This is exercised with the maj7 chord. This is a very important, very professional skill; it is in the top 2 or 3 of skills you need to know.

maj7 Patterns 1–5–10, 1–7–10: Further exercise of maj7 3-note pattern adding the 1–5–10 and 1–7–10.

Diatonic 3-note patterns with free-form textures and melodies in the right hand: Our diatonics allow us to play 3-note patterns in the left hand, and freely use any white key to form textures and releases to melody pieces in the right hand.

Blues tune example: Play the tune with left hand bass line, shells, shells to the 5th, and pulse. Use the C blues scale for the right hand, improvising freely.

Tunes: Choose a tune from one of the six at the end of the book (pages 128–151), and apply what you have learned.

Shells – Patterns from Shells
What You Will Learn

This week, we move up from the shells to the 5th of Week 1 to patterns from shells. You will learn how to take the 1–5–7 chord tones and play them as 3-note patterns.

The Video: *Week 2: Patterns from Shells 2516*

Warm Up

To get started, play through the master progression with the root in the left hand followed by the 5th in the right. This will help you in putting the 5th into memory.

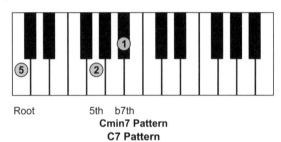

Master Progression

Once you get the fifths down, start creating 3-note patterns in the left hand playing 1–5–7, on beats 1, 2, and 3. Play through the 2516 piece on the Patterns Using Shells worksheet (page 37), playing just the patterns in your left hand. As you go through the piece, note that the 7 is a ♭7 for the min7 and dom7 chords.

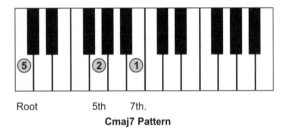

Here is an example of the first line of the 2516 piece. Notice how it shows where in each measure the root, 5, 7 are played.

- Play through the 2516 application piece on the next page. Start with simple steps.
  Level 1: Left hand only 3-note patterns.
  Level 2: Right hand melody only.
  Level 3: Left hand root with right hand melody.
  Level 4: Left hand shells with right hand melody.
  Level 5: Left hand patterns with right hand melody.
  Level 6: Fragment as needed.

Remember to pedal; it holds the tones and gives you time to set up your left hand for the upcoming pattern.

Patterns Using Shells Worksheet
2516 Application

Level 1: Left hand only 3-note patterns.

Level 2: Right hand melody only.

Level 3: Left hand root with right hand melody.

Level 4: Left hand shells with right hand melody.

Level 5: Left hand patterns with right hand melody.

Level 6: Fragment as needed.

Patterns Using Shells Worksheet

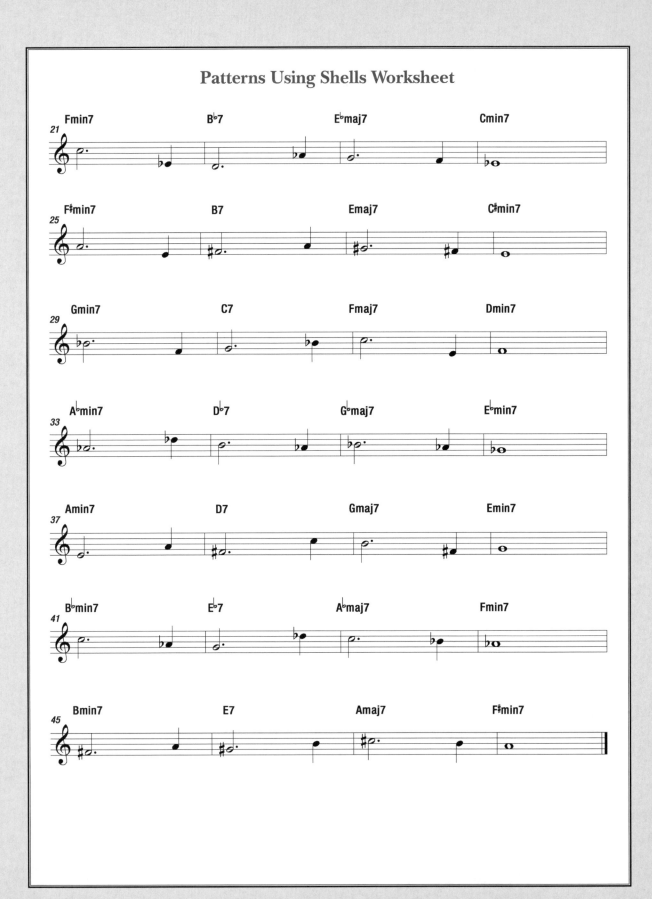

3rds: 3rds on Compression
What You Will Learn

3rds on compression is a very important concept. "On compression" means with the shell. You will use it in almost all your playing. It helps spread your chords across both of your hands. It is the foundation for more advanced playing. It is one of the top five skills in this book.

First and foremost, you need to be able to find your 3rds in all 12 keys. We covered that in week 1, and if you have troubles here, you should consider more work on the week 1 lesson.

The 3rd occurs as a natural 3rd in maj7, maj, dom7, aug7, and maj6 chords. We will be working on those chords this week. Next week, we will place emphasis on the ♭3rd and its function.

The Video: *Week 2: 3rds Applied on Compression.*

Exercise

In 3rds on compression, you add the 3rd of the chord in your right hand, under the melody note as you play the melody. Play the 3rds Applied on Compression Worksheet on page 41 (first line is shown below), starting with shells in your left hand. As you play each shell, add the 3rd under the melody note as you play the melody. In the first bar, play the shell (C–B) in the left hand and simultaneously play the melody note with the third under it (E–C) as shown in the right hand. In the example below, I have actually written in the third to let you know what to play. It is important to use this written example as an illustration; do not write the 3rds into your music.

In the second bar, the 3rd of Fmaj7 is an A, which fits just below the written C, or you could play it an octave lower if your hand spreads that far. Either is correct. When applying this type of chord building, you have to position your left hand to find the best fit for both hands on the keyboard. You may need to move your left hand down an octave to give room for your right hand. In general, you should try to keep the left hand close to the right hand as you play. It sounds more harmonious that way.

In the third bar, the 3rd of B♭maj7 is a D, but there already is a D in the melody. In this case, you can play the 3rd an octave lower. Continue on through the exercise sheet. You could continue with shells in your left hand or move up to shells to the 5th if you are comfortable. Always remember that we use the 5th as an inner tonal move, after the shell is played; this adds interest and helps keep time. Avoid playing the 1–5–7 together.

Pedaling

Pedaling is very helpful in this exercise. It allows you to keep the chord tone ringing during the 4th beat of the measure, enabling you to set up your hands for the chord and notes of the next bar. Remember that as you play, you let the pedal up at the start of a chord and place it right back down. Going up shuts off the previous tones, and putting it down sustains the current tones.

Final Comment

3rds on compression gets you playing all the four chord tones, the 1–3–5–7, spreading them across both hands. Traditional studies have students play the full chord in the left hand and the melody in the right, and eventually move to putting the 3rd into the right hand. We begin with this powerful professional layout in our chord building. This is an important technique. All advanced playing is built on this technique. Learn it and use it.

3rds Applied Worksheet
On Compression

Level 1: Play the melody alone with the Shells Left Hand.

Level 2: Apply the 3rd of the chord under the melody in Right Hand. Shell to 5th in Left Hand

> **Important:** 3rds appear on maj7, dom7, maj6, aug7

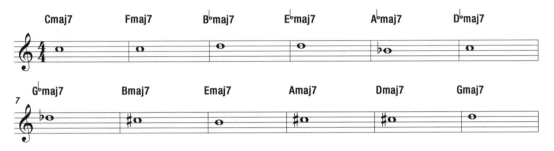

> **Important:** If the 3rd is in the melody, you can play the 3rd of the chord the octave below if you have room.

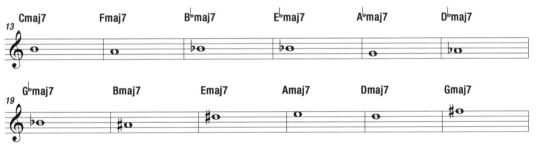

> **Important:** Observe the Left Hand Shell Placement try to get tight to Right Hand content.

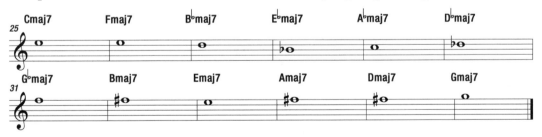

Important: If you are still unsure of the 3rds, you can isolate practice over the Progression below with Left Hand Root and Right Hand 3rd quickly through all keys.

$$C \quad F \quad B^\flat \quad E^\flat \quad A^\flat \quad D^\flat \quad G^\flat \quad B \quad E \quad A \quad D \quad G$$

$$C \quad E^\flat \quad G^\flat \quad A \quad C^\sharp \quad E \quad G \quad B^\flat \quad D \quad F \quad A^\flat \quad B$$

$$C \quad D \quad E \quad F^\sharp \quad A^\flat \quad B^\flat \quad C^\sharp \quad B \quad A \quad G \quad F \quad E^\flat$$

Patterns
What You Will Learn
Patterns will be very important parts of your playing, as they can effectively outline the chord. In this week, I build on Week 1, adding two Major 7 patterns in your left hand, the 1–5–10 and the 1–7–10. In these patterns, the 10th is the same as the 3rd, just an octave higher. These are commonly called 10th patterns on the piano.

The Video: *Week 2: Base Patterns 10ths Maj7*

Major 7th Base Patterns 1–5–10 and 1–7–10
See the Patterns: Take a look at the diagram below and notice the two patterns containing the 10th that we are adding. You can use your pinky–index finger–thumb, or your pinky–middle finger–thumb. Choose your favorite fingering for this extra stretch.

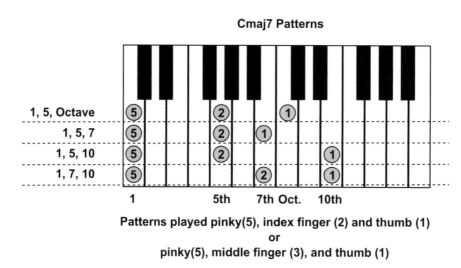

Cmaj7 Patterns

Patterns played pinky(5), index finger (2) and thumb (1)
or
pinky(5), middle finger (3), and thumb (1)

Pedal: The 1–5–10 and 1–7–10 are quite a stretch, and you probably cannot play them with your hand sitting in one position. This means you must pedal at the start of the pattern to maintain your tones; and then after playing the 1, lift and move your hand to reach the 5–10 or 7–10. Refer to the illustration below. The pedal goes down to start the first pattern, and then comes up and goes back down at the start of the next pattern. This gives you the 4th beat of the measure as a time to reposition your left hand for the upcoming pattern. Your tones are being held by the pedal, and your hands are free to move.

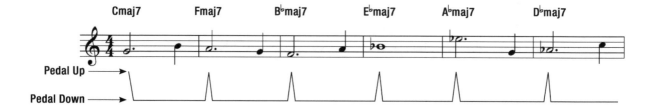

Level 1

Start by playing the 1–5–10 in your left hand by itself and cycle through all the 12 Major 7th chords using the Master Progression: Cmaj7, Fmaj7, B♭maj7, etc. Then do the same for the 1–7–10. Remember to pedal.

C F B♭ E♭ A♭ D♭ G♭ B E A D G
C E♭ G♭ A C♯ E G B♭ D F A♭ B
C D E F♯ G♯ B♭ C♯ B A G F E♭

Master Progression

Level 2

Your left hand plays the pattern and your right hand plays the melody of the work tunes for the three progressions in the Base Patterns worksheet (page 44): the Cycle 5, the Diminished, and the Whole Tone progressions. Example of the first line is below.

Play through the progressions on the worksheet using both patterns, the 1–5–10 and the 1–7–10.

Fragment—a term I use frequently in my teaching—means playing a few bars at a time until you get it down.

Level 3

Left hand plays patterns, right hand plays the 3rd on beat 4. Go through the master progression on the bottom of the second page of the worksheet. Example is shown in Level 1 below.

Level 4

Left hand plays patterns, right hand plays the 3rd on beat 1 with the start of the pattern, followed by the 3rd on beat 4 as well. Basically play, the dotted half to quarter note using the 3rd for both notes as shown in Level 2 above. Go through the master progression on the bottom of the second page of the worksheet.

Final Notes:

- Fragment
- Pedal
- Position left hand during beat 4 to be ready for upcoming pattern

Base Patterns Worksheet
1 5 10–1 7 10
(Major 7)

Left Hand	C F B♭ E♭ A♭ D♭ G♭ B E A D G
1 5 10	C E♭ G♭ A C♯ E G B♭ D F A♭ B
1 7 10	C D E F♯ G♯ B♭ C♯ B A G F E♭

Master Progression

Level 1: Left Hand Pattern by itself through all keys. (Vary order through Master Progression.)

Level 2: Work each Left Hand Pattern through the 3 progressions.

Cycle 5 Progression

Diminished Progression

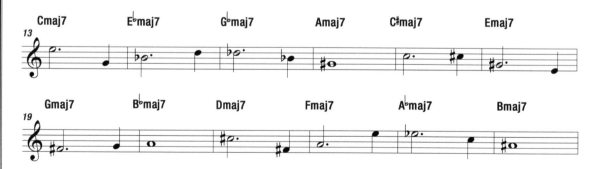

Base Patterns Worksheet
1 5 10–1 7 10

Whole Tone Progression

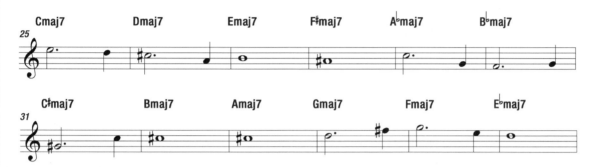

Level 3: Patterns in Left Hand, 3rd on beat 4 in the Right Hand.

Level 4: Patterns in Left Hand, 3rd on beat 1 and 3rd on beat 4 in Right Hand.

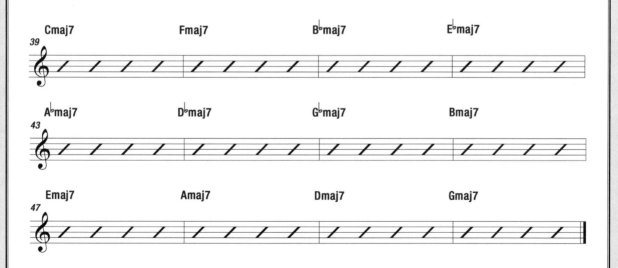

Diatonic Patterns with Texture Release
What You Will Learn

In Week 1, I introduced you to diatonic patterns. This week we will take those diatonic patterns and add textures, a more advanced right-hand concept. The lesson will help you become more comfortable with spontaneously playing textures in your right hand.

The Video: *Week2: 3-Note Patterns Texture Release*

Texture Release

Throughout the lesson, you play the 3-note pattern in your left hand, and in the right hand I introduce what I refer to as a texture, 2 notes played together with narrow and/or wide intervals (spacing between notes). The textures add interest and a nice chordal sound. The whole note texture is followed by 4 quarter notes releasing to a new 3-note pattern, along with a new whole-note texture. An example is below.

The Patterns

Cmaj7	**Dmin7**	**C/E**	**Fmaj7**	**G7**	**Amin7**	**G/B**
C G C	D A D	E C E	F C F	G D G	A E A	B G B

Level 1

Start with Level 1 by playing line 1 above, which uses a Cmaj7 releasing to a Dmin7 with a texture in the right hand. Then do line 2, which has the Cmaj7 releasing to Fmaj7. Continue with the Cmaj7 releasing to the other 6 patterns. Then repeat, using Dmin7 releasing to all the other patterns. Then repeat with C/E, Fmaj7, etc. Remember that your textures can be wide or narrow, and that the texture is composed of the key note and any other note. Also, your release can be one note down to the texture, or one note up to the texture. Remember to vary your texture between a note below the key note and a note above the key note.

Level 2

Once comfortable, move on to Level 2; link all these releases together and just continue playing, releasing to a new texture and 3-note pattern in each bar. It will be very melodic and you can explore endless opportunities. Place emphasis on your 4 quarter notes to help improve the melodic content of your playing.

Remember to keep the tempo slow. This assists you in finding the right notes, lets you explore options, and creates a very relaxed feeling for your tunes.

Watch the video at **pianoinstruction.com**

Diatonic—3-Note Patterns
Texture Release

Level 1: Start by taking just one Key Note and repeating this application with new Target as your main focal point. Not only do you see the new Target but apply a wide or narrow texture.

Level 2: Once comfortable with Level 1 isolated exercise, you can link them all together. Place emphasis on your 4 quarter notes as they will be instrumental in setting up endless possibilities.

Important: Be sure to keep the tempo very slow when applying yourself here. This is more fitting for this type of relaxed playing and keeping tempos slow will enable you to see things you are playing even more clearly.

Linking Between Chords
The Target Notes will help develop a seamless connection in your improvised line.

*Observe both Target options (above and below) when setting up Target notes.

Curley's Blues up to 3rds
What You Will Learn

Now we are going to have some fun applying the techniques you have learned to a blues tune that I have written.

The Video: *Week 2: Curley's Blues up to 3rds*

Get comfortable playing the tune using shells or shell to the 5th in the left hand. The tune is written in the key of C, so the C blues scale will work against it. Once you get comfortable with playing the tune, move on to substituting the C blues scale for the tune.

Level 1

Bass Line in Left Hand: Start with the tune in the right hand and a single-note bass line only in the left hand. The bass line is formed by playing just the root of the chord and playing it an octave lower than normal. Remember to go slow; it's easier, and it makes it sound more bluesy.

Level 2

Shells and Shells to the 5th: After using the bass line, you can move up to shells in the left hand and then shells to the 5th. Shells to the 5th is nice because it develops a rhythm for the tune. You can even get more rhythmic by pulsing the shells. Keep on going until you are comfortable.

Later, in week 4, you can return here and start adding in the 3rd to the right hand.

Level 3

C Blues Scale: When you have the melody down, you can turn to the C blues scale and start improvising. Count 1 + 2 + 3 + 4 +; basically 8 notes per bar. Start by moving up and down the keyboard with the C blues scale. Then try some rocking back and forth with the same two notes. Then rock and climb up, rock and climb down. You can even mix in repeating the same note over and over. Play around, just move around without leaping all over the place.

Tunes: Choose a tune from one of the six at the end of the book (pages 127–151) and apply what you have learned.

Enjoy yourself.

Curley's Blues

Level 1: Root Bass Notes in Left Hand, melody in Right Hand.
Level 2: Shells or Shells to the 5th in the Left Hand and melody in the Right Hand.
Level 3: C Blues Scale.

Improvisation

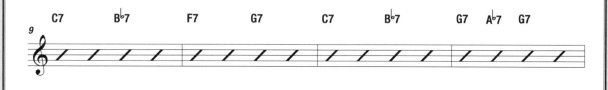

Week 2 Review

Let's review what you learned this week.

Shells

- Can you create a 3-note pattern using the root, 5th, 7th for all chords in the 2516 progression?
- Can you find the 5th in the right hand for all chords in the 2516 progression piece?

3rds

- Can you explain 3rds on compression?
- Can you apply 3rds on compression to the maj7 Whole Note worksheet?

Patterns

- Can you play the 1–5–10 and 1–7–10 patterns for all maj7 chords?
- Can you play the maj7 work pieces using the 1, 5, 10 pattern?
- Can you play the maj7 work pieces using the 1, 7, 10 pattern?
- Can you play the patterns on the Master Progression work piece, inserting the 3rd in your right hand Level 1? Level 2?

3-Note Patterns Texture Release

- Can you play the 3-Note diatonic patterns with Texture Release, one line at a time?
- Can you play the 3-Note diatonic patterns with Texture Release, stringing them together for 5 minutes?

Curley's Blues

- Can you play *Curley's Blues* with bass line, shells, and shells to the 5th?
- Can you play *Curley's Blues* with the C Blues Scale?

Tunes

- Can you play a tune from the back of the book using shells, shells to the 5th, and patterns?

Week 3

Skills You Will Learn in Week 3

The ♭3rd: The ♭3rd is a very important tone in a chord and will bring forth the minor quality of the chordal sound. ♭3rd on compression is covered. Exercises will have you adding the ♭3rd to a tune of whole notes, and to a tune of dotted half note to quarter note pairs.

Slash Chords: The shell lesson will explain slash chords, and how to play shells, shell to the 5th, and 3-note patterns with slash chords.

min7 Patterns: min7 patterns are introduced utilizing the ♭10th in your left hand and the ♭3rd and ♭10th in the right. You will play through 2516 progressions with the chord changes, min7 to maj7, exercising your 3rd and ♭3rd knowledge.

Diatonic freeform with no key notes: This week, we break away from having to focus on key notes for each chord. I will have you freeform playing, and you decide whether to play key notes or not, just moving up and down the keyboard creating your own enjoyable music. You will do scale tones, leaps, and wandering.

Blues tune example: You will play *Blues for Calliope* with single-note bass line, shells, and shells to the 5th. You will apply 3rds on compression, an advanced skill. You will play the C blues scale on the piece.

Tunes: Choose a tune from the back of the book (pages 127–151) or try one of your own favorites.

Shells: Slash Chords

What Is a Slash Chord?

A slash chord has the form C/E. It looks complicated but is actually pretty simple. Chords such as C/E mean that you have a C chord with E in the bass. I like to read it as C *but* E in the bass. The left side of the slash describes the chord, and the right side is the bass note to be played in your left hand. When you play a slash chord, you play the bass note as the root with the chord above the bass note.

The Video: *Week 3: Understanding Slash Chords*

Left-Hand Options

Slash-Chord Shell: In my method, I play a slash-chord shell by playing octaves: the bass note, and the bass note one octave higher. It is like my shell, played with pinky and thumb; and it is 2 bass notes an octave apart, as shown below.

C/E "Shell"

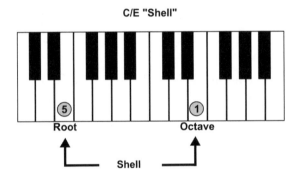

Slash-Chord Shell to Chord Tone: Very much like the shell to the 5th that you have learned, slash chords can be played with slash chord shell to a chord tone. The shell is, as I just mentioned, two bass notes separated by an octave, and you play it on beat one. On beat 3, you add in any chord tone from the chord specified in the slash chord. Very often the easiest choice is the root of the chord. So in our example of C/E, the notes to be played would be E C E. You might notice that we have already used this in our diatonics lessons in the cases of C/E and G/B.

C/E "Shell to Chord Tone"

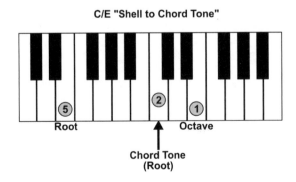

3-Note Pattern: The 3-note pattern for a slash chord follows the same rule: bass note–chord tone–bass note. Thus for C/E, the pattern would be E C E. It is not easy to find patterns analogous to 1 5 10; every slash chord has different relationship of chord to bass note. The best approach is to stick with bass note–chord root–bass note. Once you are comfortable with chord tones, if you do find something you like, pencil it in.

C/E "3-Note Pattern"

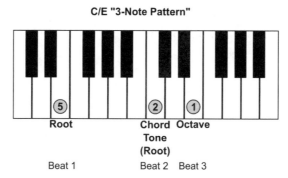

Right-Hand Options: Chord Tones
============

Right-Hand Options: Chord Tones

The chord tones for a slash chord are the chord tones for the chord specified before the slash. The bass note is not necessarily added in as a chord tone, but it is not excluded either. If it happens to be a chord tone of the chord, it is a chord tone. So just focus on the chord and use its chord tones.

C/E chord tones would be the 1 3 5 of C major, or C E G.

C7/B♭ chord tones would be the 1 3 5 ♭7 of C7, or C E G B♭.

A Word on Triads

Triads of chords like a major chord or a minor, or basically any kind of chord without a suffix like 7 or 6 or 7♭5, etc., are just the 1 3 5 chord tones of the chord, because there is no additional suffix specified. Remember that the 3 or the 5 must be adjusted flat or sharp depending on the rule of the chord type (e.g., minor chords have a flat 3rd).

Exercise

Level 1: Play through the Understanding Slash Chords worksheet (page 54) starting with just your left hand playing the shell (bass note–bass note octave). Then add in the right-hand melody. Note that in bars 7 and 8, I have embellished a bit by playing all the chord tones of the slash chord in the melody.

Level 2: Play through the piece with shell to chord tone in your left hand.

Level 3: Play through the piece with 3-note patterns in your left hand.

Level 4: If desired, when you need a challenge, throw in a few chord tones in your right hand below the melody. Look for places with not a lot going on in the melody, like bars with 2 half notes or a whole note. I call this "filling in" in the video.

Understanding Slash Chords

Level 1: Left Hand Shell Only, then Shell and melody.

Level 2: Left Hand Shell to chord tone, Right Hand melody.

Level 3: Left Hand Patterns, Right Hand melody.

Level 4: Optional, add chord tones in the Right Hand.

Triad formation notated here – try building your own on other chords.

♭3rd on Compression

This lesson continues our 3rd on Compression lessons with exercises on the ♭3rd. The 3rd is flat on the following chords:

Minor   minor7   min7♭5   min6   dim7

In this lesson we will only be working on the min7, but this will give you the practice you need finding the ♭3rd. Watch for the other chord types in your own tunes.

The Video: *Week 3: ♭3rd Applied on Compression*

Level 1: Finding the ♭3rd

You should start by just finding the ♭3rd. This is an echo of the lesson we had in week 1, when we first saw the ♭3rd. Go through the master progression and play the root in your left hand, followed by the ♭3rd in your right. This should warm you up.

C F B♭ E♭ A♭ D♭ G♭ B E A D G

C E♭ G♭ A C♯ E G B♭ D F A♭ B

C D E F♯ G♯ B♭ C♯ B A G F E♭

Master Progression

Level 2: Whole Note Exercise

Play through the ♭3rds Applied on Compression Worksheet (page 57). Start with shell to the 5th in your left hand, and in your right hand play the melody, adding the ♭3rd of the chord placed below the melody note. The ♭3rd is played on the compression of the chord. The first exercise is all whole notes in the right hand, so you have a lot of time to think and plan your next note. In the example below, I have included that ♭3rd below the melody note. This should get you started. Keep your left hand close to your right hand as you play; this will cause all the tones to blend together evenly between the two hands. It sounds much smoother this way.

Start with bar 1, where an E♭ is added on compression below the melody note of C. Continue on. In bar 5, you could put the ♭3rd right next to the melody note as shown, or you could add it an octave lower. You might have to move your left hand down to accomplish this.

After getting up to speed with the example, start playing from the exercise sheet where you have to come up with the ♭3rd by yourself. Do not write the 3rds into the music, and no peeking back at the example. Your goal is to find the 3rds as you play, not by reading them from a music sheet. In bar 8, Bmin7, the melody note is already a ♭3rd. This will happen a lot. Just add another ♭3rd an octave lower.

If you need to make it easier, ease back on your left-hand difficulty by playing only shells, or root. Remember that the ♭3rd appears in more than just the min7; be aware of minor, min7♭5, min6, dim 7 as well.

Level 3: Dotted Half Note to Quarter Note Exercise

When comfortable with the whole notes, increase the difficulty by playing dotted half to quarter in the right hand. The example below has the ♭3rds written in for the first few bars. Get started with this, then do the whole exercise sheet.

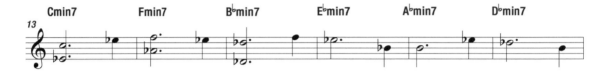

As you play this melody, use shell to the 5th, and your hands and mind will get a workout. You will be playing the shell and the melody note and the ♭3rd on the first beat, the 5th in the left hand on beat 3, and finally the quarter note melody note in the right hand on beat 4. When you get this down, it will be spectacular.

Prepare for Each New Piece

Whenever you pick up a new piece, look carefully at all the chords to be used and at which chords will receive the 3rd and ♭3rd. You already should be doing this for the 7th with 1 note down–2 notes down–3 notes down, as well as the 5th. Now just add the 3rd to your preparation. Of course, in this exercise it is easy because they are all ♭3rds, but in playing your own tunes you will find a mix.

Final Notes:
- Remember to pedal.
- This is one of the top three skills of the book; master it, enjoy it.

♭3rds Applied On Compression Worksheet

Applying the ♭3rd on the Compression (with the Shell) is a very important part of our harmonic layout of chords in tunes. You must know the 3rds in all keys and then this will make the ♭3rd easier to see. It is essential to know the 3rds and ♭3rds of all keys quickly off the top of your head.

The ♭3rd will indicate the chord is minor tonality and it is important to fully understand as to which chord will use the 3rd and which the ♭3rd. We have already addressed the Shells and the 5th and how they adjust to fit almost all chords to get comfortable with this very important tone.

Level 1: Play Master Progression, root in Left Hand, 3rd in Right Hand.
Level 2: Play Whole Note Melody with ♭3rd on compression.
Level 3: Play Dotted Half to Quarter Melody with ♭3rd on compression.

Important: Memorize these common chord types the ♭3rd work on. Our example below is using just min7.

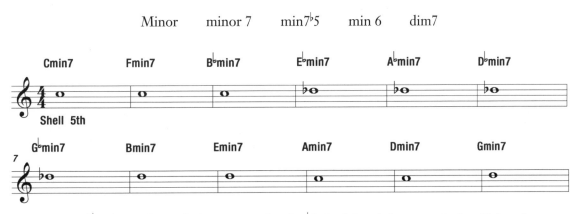

Important: If ♭3rd is in the melody you can play the ♭3rd of chord the octave below if there's room.

Minor 7th Patterns

This lesson is very similar to last week's major 7th patterns, except we are working on the minor 7th patterns. What's the difference? You use a flat 7 for the 7th, and you use a flat 3 for the 3rd (and therefore a flat 10 for the 10th).

The Video: *Week 3: Minor 7 Base Patterns*

Left Hand Choices: The left hand should play one of the 3-note patterns. Start with 1–5–octave, as it is the same as a maj7 with none of the new flats; then move on as comfortable.

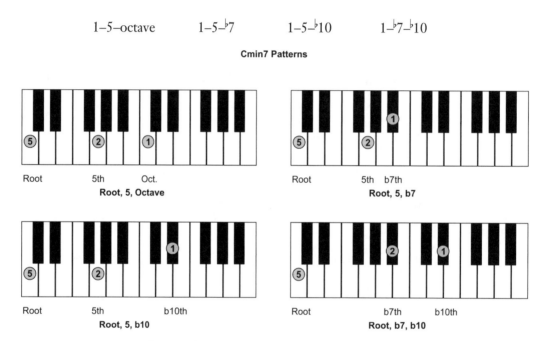

Patterns played pinky (5), index finger (2) and thumb (1)

Level 1

Start by playing the patterns alone in your left hand. Begin with 1–5–octave. Cycle through all of the 12 minor 7th chords using the master progression: e.g., Cmin7, Fmin7, B♭min7. When comfortable, move on to the other three patterns.

C	F	B♭	E♭	A♭	D♭	G♭	B	E	A	D	G
C	E♭	G♭	A	C♯	E	G	B♭	D	F	A♭	B
C	D	E	F♯	G♯	B♭	C♯	B	A	G	F	E♭

Master Progression

Level 2

Play the Minor 7th Worksheet (page 60). It is a dotted half to quarter note melody. Play it first using 1–5–octave. Move through the other left-hand patterns as comfortable. Then mix up the patterns. Remember to pedal. Fragment and repeat bars when necessary. Sample on next page.

Level 3

Move on to the Minor7–Major7 alternating worksheet (page 60), which will alternate between ♭3rds (and ♭10ths) and natural 3rds, as well as ♭7ths and natural 7ths. Work through the piece with the patterns, note that the 1–5–octave does not change going from min7 to maj7. Example below.

Level 4

Using the Minor7–Major7 alternating worksheet, play with patterns in the left hand and replace the right-hand melody with playing the 3rd as whole notes on compression. Remember to adjust the 3rd to a ♭3rd in your right hand for the min7 chords. Example below.

Then play dotted half to quarter notes in your left hand, using the 3rd for both notes as in the example below.

Finally, play the melody for a few bars, then substitute the 3rds for a bar, and then back to the melody.

Final Notes:

- Get comfortable mixing the min7 with the maj7.
- Go slow, go smooth, always be looking ahead and try to connect the measures evenly.
- Pedal.
- Use beat 4 to position your left hand for the upcoming pattern.
- Fragment as needed.
- Adjust 3rd to ♭3rd where needed in right-hand play.

Minor 7th Worksheet
Base Patterns

Octave Range and 10th Range—Patterns when applied will take on many shapes. Here we look at my core base patterns which like out maj7 chords will be built around Octave Range and 10th Range. These 4 will be easier if you are comfortable with the maj7 application before adjusting to fit the min7 chord type.

Octave Range	**Level 1** LH—Root 5th Octave	**Level 2** LH—Root 5th ♭7th	
10th Range	**Level 3** LH—Root 5th ♭10	**Level 4** LH—Root ♭7th ♭10	

Level 1: Play patterns through the Master Progression Left Hand only.
Level 2: Play Minor7 Workpiece with mixed patterns.
Level 3: Play Minor7-Major7 Workpiece with mixed patterns.
Level 1: Play Minor7-Major7 Workpiece with patterns and 3rds on compression.

Minor 7th Workpiece

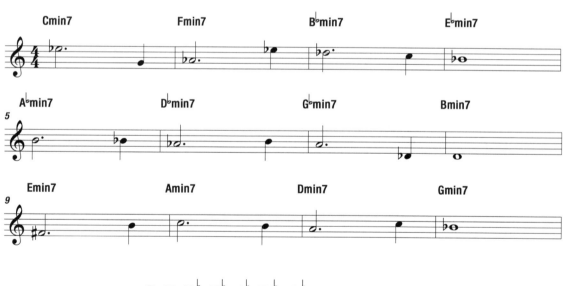

Master Progression

Minor 7th–Major 7th Worksheet
Base Patterns

Minor7—Major7 Alternating

Here we focus on alternating between maj7 and min7 chords in a musical 4-chord progression that will run you through all keys for both chord types.

3rd ♭3rd Application

I strongly recommend you to play the Alternating Progression with just the 3rds applied against each chord. This is a fun way to really learn a very important note that we will be using in all our playing.

As Written, Then 3rd

This is a creative application where I have you play a bar as written and on the up and coming chord play the 3rd for that bar. You can randomly select which bars you would like to place in your 3rd.

Diatonic Patterns: No Key Notes
What You Will Learn

In this diatonic lesson, we are going to play any white note in your right hand, letting you put together very musical melodies. We will simplify your left hand to just two chord groupings, playing them back and forth as we experiment with freeform white-note melodies in your right hand.

The Video: *Week 3: Diatonic Patterns RH Free Form 2 Chord Groupings*

Level 1: Two Chord Groupings

Play two chord groupings, as shown on the Diatonic Patterns Worksheet (page 64). The first is pair is Cmaj7 and Dmin7. Repeat the pairs, back and forth, in your left hand as you explore in your right hand. Alternating between the two chords helps you gain control and develop musical ideas.

Right-Hand Scales

As you are playing two chord groupings in your left hand, play some scale ideas in your right hand, slowly up and down the keyboard as shown in the example below. Play the sample to hear what I am talking about, then go beyond the example and create your own scale ideas.

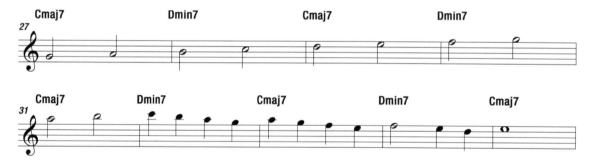

Level 2: Right-Hand Leaps

Add some leaps in the right hand. Leaps will add melodic interest in your improvisational ideas. Play some scale ideas followed by a leap. When leaping, it is always advised to stay close following the leap. Try not to do two consecutive leaps, because it adds a broken quality to your music. Leap, play scale ideas, leap, play scale ideas. Take a look at the example below.

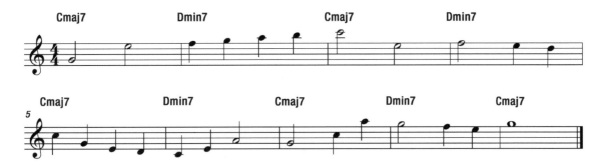

Play through all the chord pairs listed on the bottom of the exercise sheet.

Wander

Wander all around the keyboard with your right hand. Keep the tempo slow and relaxed, and adjust your right hand to meet those inner challenges you may have. Alter the tempo, string some sixteenth notes together. Go wild. Get musical. Play at your comfort level, or challenge yourself. Throw in some textures. As you play with the different chord pairs, listen to hear what notes sound good and what don't. Try to learn from what you play; remember those techniques and combinations that you liked.

Watch the video to see what I do. This is a fun exercise.

Level 3: All Chord Groups

Play through all of the chord groups listed at the bottom of the page. Use the Cmaj7 chord groups as a model for the others.

Diatonic Patterns Worksheet
Right Hand Free Form
2 Chord Groupings

Level 1: Begin with the Cmaj7 (2 chord groupings) as displayed. Become comfortable using scale motion to start.

Level 2: Take the Cmaj (2 chord groupings) and now add leaps within your line.

Important: Use the Cmaj7 (chord groupings) as reference for the other groupings.

Level 3: Move onto the next 2 chord groupings and repeat the above process.

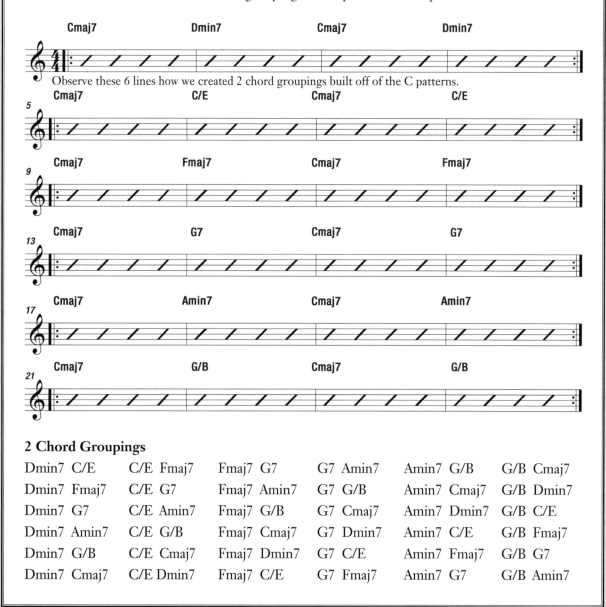

Observe these 6 lines how we created 2 chord groupings built off of the C patterns.

2 Chord Groupings

Dmin7 C/E	C/E Fmaj7	Fmaj7 G7	G7 Amin7	Amin7 G/B	G/B Cmaj7
Dmin7 Fmaj7	C/E G7	Fmaj7 Amin7	G7 G/B	Amin7 Cmaj7	G/B Dmin7
Dmin7 G7	C/E Amin7	Fmaj7 G/B	G7 Cmaj7	Amin7 Dmin7	G/B C/E
Dmin7 Amin7	C/E G/B	Fmaj7 Cmaj7	G7 Dmin7	Amin7 C/E	G/B Fmaj7
Dmin7 G/B	C/E Cmaj7	Fmaj7 Dmin7	G7 C/E	Amin7 Fmaj7	G/B G7
Dmin7 Cmaj7	C/E Dmin7	Fmaj7 C/E	G7 Fmaj7	Amin7 G7	G/B Amin7

Blues Tunes: *Blues for Calliope*

Play through the tune as written, at various levels, moving through shells in your left hand and then to shells to the 5th. Refer to the Blues for Calliope Worksheet on page 67.

The Video: *Week 3: Blues for Calliope up to 3rds*

Level 1: Root in Left Hand

Play the root of the chord in your left hand. Play it low to give it a cool bass tone. Melody in your right.

Level 2: Shells

Play shells in the left hand, melody in your right.

Level 3: Shells to the 5th

Play shells to the 5th in your left hand, melody in your right.

Level 4: 3rd on Compression

Play shells to the 5th in your left hand, and 3rds on Compression in your right. This is an advanced technique that you can explore now that you have had some lessons on the 3rd. You will learn more about it in later weeks. 3rd on Compression means you add the 3rd of the chord to the melody in your right hand as you start the chord. Place the 3rd below the melody note. An example is shown below. If this is too difficult for you now, wait until we cover the technique in depth in later weeks.

Remember, do not pencil in the 3rds. I have included them in the graphic as an explanation, a way of documenting to you what (and where) I mean by 3rds on compression. In real application, you should be determining these 3rds on the fly, and you will succeed only if you learn to do it on the fly.

Level 5: C Blues Scale

Once you get comfortable, start using the C blues scale. Make sure you are very comfortable with your left hand before starting the blues scale, because with the blues scale you want to keep a steady rhythm of time.

When you are playing the blues scale, you want to play with a steady tempo of eighth notes. Count 1 + 2 + 3 + 4 + ... Keep it steady and run up and down the keyboard.

If you need, you can start with quarter notes, or even whole notes.

You can rock two notes, or repeat a note multiple times. Switch between options. Play around. Most of all, keep that steady beat going. Remember, your blues scale will help keep the time moving in the piece and help define the time in every measure you play.

Blues for Calliope

Level 1: Root in Left Hand, melody in Right Hand.

Level 2: Shells in Left Hand, melody in Right Hand.

Level 3: Shells to the 5th in Left Hand, melody in Right Hand.

Level 4: Shells to the 5th in Left Hand, 3rds on compression in Right Hand.

Level 5: Shells to the 5th in Left Hand, C blues scale in Right Hand.

Improvisation

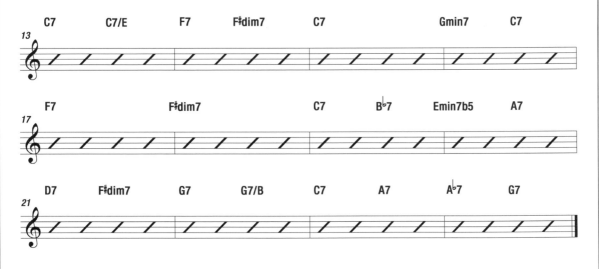

Week 3 Review

Shells

- Can you describe the parts of a slash chord?
- Can you play the shell of a slash chord?
- Can you play the shell to the 5th of a slash chord?
- Can you play the 10th pattern of a slash chord?
- Do you know the chord tones of a slash chord?

3rds

- Do you know what chord types have a ♭3rd?
- Can you play 3rds on compression with min7 chords in the whole-note work piece?
- Can you play 3rds on compression with min7 chords in the dotted-half to quarter-note work piece?

Patterns

- Do you know the adjustments for the four minor7 patterns?
- Can you play all four minor7 patterns through the master progression?
- Can you play the minor7 work piece?
- Can you play the minor7–major7 alternating workpiece?

Diatonic Patterns

- Can you play freeform right-hand melodies against the diatonic patterns?

Blues for Calliope

- Can you play *Blues for Calliope* with shells to the 5th in your right hand?
- Can you play *Blues for Calliope* with 3rds on compression in your right hand?
- Can you play *Blues for Calliope* with the C Blues Scale?

Tunes

- Can you play one of the supplied tunes, or one of your own favorites using:
  1. Shells
  2. Shells to the 5th
  3. Patterns
  4. 3rds on compression

Week 4

Skills You Will Learn in Week 4

3rds & ♭3rds on Compression: 3rds on compression is one of our most important skills. It is one of the top three techniques taught in this book. Exercises with 2516 progressions will challenge you with a mix of 3rds and ♭3rds. Master this lesson and you will be close to attaining your next level of playing.

Stride: Introduction to the 10th stride, a powerful left-hand technique. Play the stride against maj7 chords.

♭3rd and ♭7th in patterns in the left hand: Exercise 3-note patterns for maj7, min7, dom7 chords. Use the 1 5 7 10, 1 5 7 ♭10, and 1 5 ♭7 ♭10 left-hand patterns. Become comfortable with adjusting chord tones for different chord types.

Diatonics: Exercise four chord groupings with textures and freeform playing in the right hand.

Tunes: Choose a tune from one of the six at the end of the book (pages 127–151) or one of your favorites, and play using shells, shells to the 5th, patterns, and 3rds on compression.

3rds: 3rds & ♭3rds on Compression 2516 Exercise
What You Will Learn This Week

The 2516 progression used in this week's exercises contains 3rds and ♭3rds, thus making for a good workout of your skills. The progressions contain a min7, dom7, maj7, and min7. The min7 contains a ♭3rd while the dom7 and maj7 contain natural 3rds.

The Video: *Week 4: 3rds on Compression 2516*

Level 1

Play through the 2516 Progression Worksheet (page 71) with shells in your left hand and the melody in your right.

Level 2

Play through the worksheet with shells to the 5th in your left hand and the melody in your right.

Level 3

Play through the worksheet with shells to the 5th in your left hand and the melody in your right. Place the 3rd of the chord on compression below the melody note right under each chord. See the example on the first line below.

Play through the worksheet; keep your left hand near your right hand. Finding the correct position for your left hand takes a little thought; too close and you overlap and collide, too far apart and the tones don't blend.

In bar 4, your left hand could be very close to your right, overlapping a little, or you could move it down an octave.

Bar 6, the F♯7, has the 3rd already in the melody. Add another 3rd an octave below. This also occurs in bar 7.

Pedaling

Remember your pedaling; the pedal comes up as the chord goes down, then pedal goes immediately back down. Reposition your left hand for the upcoming chord on beat 4.

Look Ahead

Always look ahead to the next bar so you can prepare yourself for the chord and the 3rd.

Get comfortable with this technique; it is a very professional skill and one of the top three presented in this book. It will be a foundation of your playing in the future.

2516 Progression Worksheet
3rd and ♭3rd Application
On Compression

Level 1: Left Hand Shell and Right Hand melody.

Level 2: Left Hand Shell to 5th and Right Hand melody.

Level 3: Add the 3rd on compression with the Right Hand.

2516 Progression Worksheet

Stride: 10th Stride Formation Maj7

What You Will Learn This Week

This week introduces you to the 10th stride for maj7 chords. Learn this left-hand technique and how to play and pedal it.

The Video: *Week 4: 10th Stride Maj7*

The Stride

The Stride is a left-hand technique related to the shell to the 5th in that it outlines the chord and establishes time in your playing. The stride is accomplished in your left hand by playing the root (pinky) on beat 1, and then on beat 3 moving your hand up to the 7–10 pair (index–thumb). The graphic below illustrates the stride notes.

I suggest you watch the video at www.pianoinstruction.com to see the hand movement used for the stride.

Big Hands? Do you need big hands to reach the 10th in the stride? No, because you move your hand after playing the root, while the pedal is holding the root tone.

Pedaling: Pedaling is very important in the stride, to keep the tone ringing as you move your hand from root to 7–10. Remember it's an opposite effect. Let the pedal up as you play the root. Then immediately put it back down to hold the root tone as you move your hand up to the 7–10.

Exercises: Level 1

Play the maj7 stride through the master progression. Your left hand plays the stride, root to 7–10 on beats 1 and 3. When you are comfortable, add any chord tone in your right hand on beat 1.

C F B♭ E♭ A♭ D♭ G♭ B E A D G
C E♭ G♭ A C♯ E G B♭ D F A♭ B
C D E F♯ A♭ B♭ C♯ B A G F E♭

Master Progression

Level 2

Play the three pieces on the 10th Stride Formation Worksheet (page 75), stride in your left hand and melody in your right. If you want to simplify to start, play only the first note of the melody for each bar. When comfortable, move up to the full melody in your right hand. Practice on the example line below before moving up to the full worksheet.

Final Notes:

- Stretch out your left hand
- Know the 10th
- Keep it slow
- Pedal
- Try alternating 1 bar stride and 1 bar shell to the 5th
- Watch the video

10th Stride Formation Worksheet
Root–7, 10 (Maj7)

Large Hand or Not? The 10th Stride Formation is a very powerful application, often perceived to be applied by someone with very large hands. This is not always true because the Root is played followed by the 7–10 together. It does, however, frame a large space and sound on the piano.

Shell to 5th Similar Function! Observe closely how the 10th Stride Formation will have the same effect in the music as the Shell to 5th. Both create a steady flow of time and chord support.

Level 1: Left Hand plays stride through the Master Progression.
Level 1+: Add any chord tone in Right Hand on beat 1.
Level 2: Left Hand plays Stride, Right Hand plays melody on worksheet page 2.
Level 2 Simplified: Simplify Right Hand to only first note of each bar.

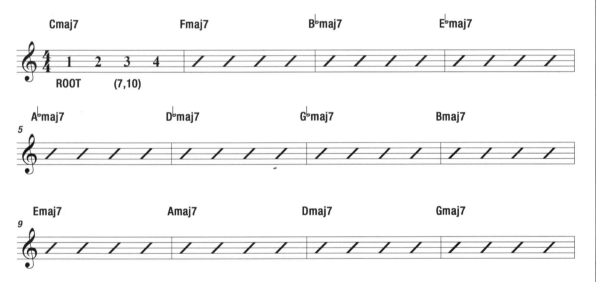

Pedaling: It is a great place to work on effective pedal technique. Isolate the Left Hand alone and remember at the beginning of each Root to be played for the new chord, the pedal comes up to shut off the prior sounds and immediately goes back down to hold the new sounds.

Think Opposite—Root Down—Pedal Up—Right Back Down

C F B♭ E♭ A♭ D♭ G♭ B E A D G

C E♭ G♭ A C♯ E G B♭ D F A♭ B

C D E F♯ G♯ B♭ C♯ B A G F E♭

Master Progression

10th Stride Formation Worksheet

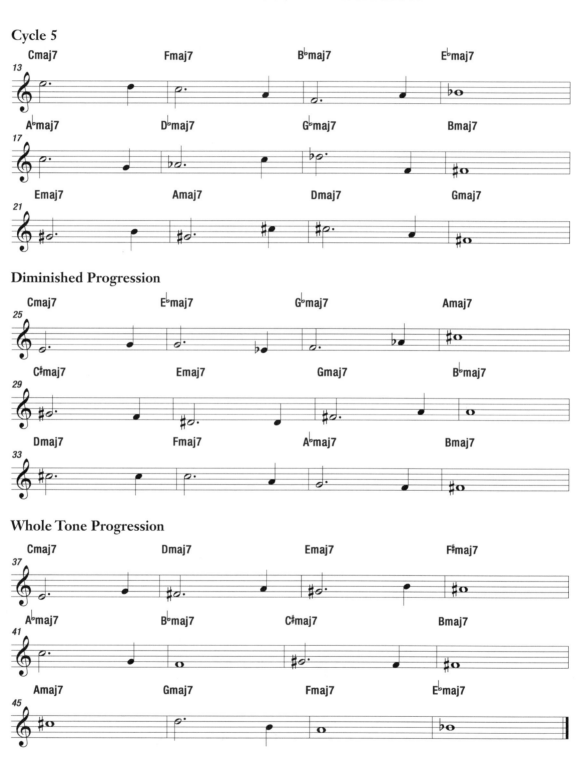

Patterns: 3-Note Patterns 2516 Against a Melody
What You Will Learn This Week

You will learn the base pattern for the dom7 chord and will be given a half note, quarter note, quarter note melody to exercise.

The Video: *Week 4: Dom7 Base Patterns and 2516*

The Dom7 Pattern

This week we are exercising the Dom7 pattern, which has a ♭7. The patterns for the dom7 are

$$1–5–\text{octave} \qquad 1–5–{}^\flat7 \qquad 1–5–10 \qquad 1–{}^\flat7–10$$

Note that the 1–5–♭7 and the 1–♭7–10 are the two patterns that contain the defining note (♭7) for dom7. Because of this, I like to use either of these two patterns when playing dom7 chords. The other patterns work, but they don't bring out the essential sound of the dom7 unless the ♭7 is somewhere in the melody in your right hand.

This week we introduce using half note, quarter, quarter in the right hand. This is a little more action than previous weeks, and it will be good practice for you.

Level 1: Master Progression

Start by playing the patterns alone in your left hand. Begin with 1–5–♭7. Cycle through all of the 12 dom7 chords using the Master Progression. When comfortable, move on to the 1–♭7–10 pattern.

C F B♭ E♭ A♭ D♭ G♭ B E A D G

C E♭ G♭ A C♯ E G B♭ D F A♭ B

C D E F♯ G♯ B♭ C♯ B A G F E♭

Master Progression

Level 2: Dom7 Workpiece

Play the Dom7 Workpiece (page 79) starting with the 1–5–♭7 pattern in your left hand. Your right hand plays the melody. Example line below.

- Fragment, playing a few bars at a time until you are comfortable.
- Simplify if you need an easier challenge to start; play only the first note of the melody for each bar, then move up to the full melody.
- Vary your patterns in your left hand.

Level 3: 2516 Workpiece

The 2516 Progression Worksheet (page 79) cycles you through all keys using three chord types. Each chord type requires different adjustments for the chord tones as show below.

maj7	min 7	dom7
1–3–5–7	1–♭3–5–♭7	1–3–5–♭7

Start with one pattern like the 1–5–octave and play the first line. Then go on to the next. In the 2516 progression workpiece, each line is an example of the 2516. Get comfortable with the line before moving on to the next. Example below.

Start mixing the patterns.

Last Notes:

- ♭7 defines the dom7.
- 2516 progression exercises your knowledge of adjustments for maj7, min7, and dom7 in all keys, and prepares you with a foundation to adapt to all the other chord types you will encounter.
- Pedal.
- Fragment.
- Simplify.

2516 Progression Worksheet
Base Patterns

Octave Range and 10th Range—Patterns when applied will take on many shapes. Here we look at my base core patterns on dom7, which like our maj7 chords will be built around Octave Range and the 10th Range. These 4 will be easier to put together if you are comfortable with the maj7 application.

Octave Range LH—Root 5th Octave
LH—Root 5th ♭7th

10th Range LH—Root 5th 10
LH—Root ♭7th 10

Mix Ranges Mix the Octave with the 10th Range for each bar.

Level 1: Left Hand plays each of the dom7 patterns through Master Progression.
Level 2: Left Hand plays patterns on dom7 Workpiece, Right Hand plays melody. Simplify fragment if necessary.

Dom7 Workpiece

2516 Progression Worksheet
2516 Workpiece

Level 3: Play all 4 patterns on 2516 Workpiece, Right Hand plays the melody. Vary patterns and watch the chord tone adjustments as you move through the different kinds of chords.

2516 Progression Worksheet

2516 Workpiece

Diatonic Patterns 4 Chord Groups with Freeform and Textures

What You Will Learn This Week

In this Diatonic lesson, I stress more freedom in your right hand, using textures and freeform improvisation to let you build your own pretty melodies. The lesson is all about the right hand and allowing it to explore freeform concepts. The left hand will play and repeat the groups of four chords using 3-note patterns, letting your right hand explore at will.

The Video: *Week 4: Diatonic Patterns 4 Chord Freeform and Textures*

Exercise

Start with the first line of the Diatonic Patterns Worksheet, example below, and play 3-note patterns in the left hand; let your right hand play freely. Any collection of white notes works except a few situations where void notes are recognized. Start with a single note per bar for a few bars, and then start stringing together groups of notes with interesting rhythms. Keep repeating the line of four chords and exploring melodies.

Try the next line with a new set of four chords. Play some two-note textures, one texture per bar. Then mix in some single-note freeform.

Void Notes

When doing freeform, you will periodically run across a void note. You will hear it: it sounds like it doesn't fit. The way to deal with void notes is to quickly resolve them one note higher or lower. Then it sounds good. Don't sit on the void note: resolve it.

Final Notes

- Play through each of the eight patterns and have some fun.
- Resolve the void notes.
- Watch the video for some ideas and inspiration.

Diatonic Patterns Worksheet
4 Chord "Free Form" & "Textures"

For this lesson, we focus on using our Diatonic Patterns through 4-bar progressions I have written. We will apply single note Free Form ideas over the 4 bars and also work on seeing the 2-Note Textures clearly. Work on 1 line, repeating it with an abundance of ideas you can put out. Then you can blend a couple of lines together and eventually connect them all.

Level 1: Improvise using Single Note ideas on one 4 bar progression at a time.
Level 2: Improvise working on 2-Note Textures thinking wide and narrow.
Level 3: Mix the Single Notes and 2-Note Textures and variety of rhythms.

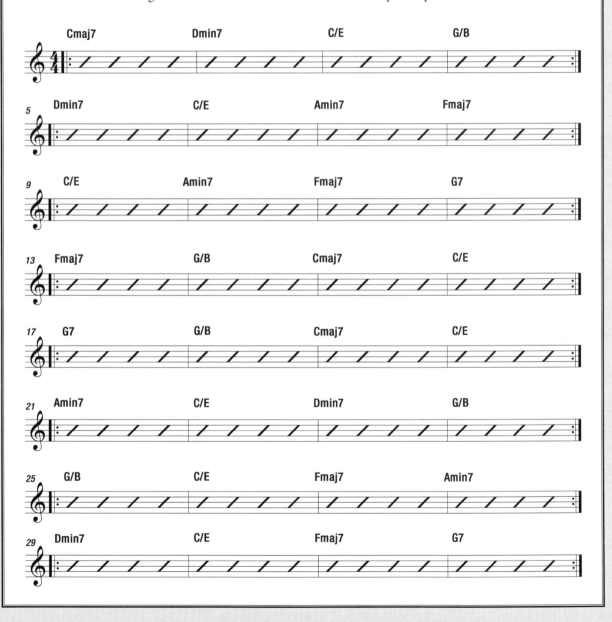

West Street Blues

Here is another fun blues piece that I have put together for you.

The Video: *Week 4:* West Street Blues *up to 3rds on Compression*

Level 1

Start off by getting to know the tune. Play the chord roots in your left hand. Play them low, like a single-note bass line. In your right hand, play the tune. It is really important to get this right, so go slow.

Level 2

After getting it down, try pulsing the shells in your left hand as you play. Eventually move up to Shells to the 5th in your left hand.

Level 3

When comfortable with the tune, try doing 3rds on compression. You have been working on 3rds on compression, so this is a good time to use those skills. In your left hand you can play Shells or shells to the 5th, or even the root bass line. Use whatever left-hand option you are comfortable with that allows you to put in the 3rd on compression.

Level 4

When done with 3rds on compression, move on to the C blues scale. Choose the left-hand option that feels comfortable today. Start one note per chord in the right hand. Then play the blues scale up and down the keyboard. Rock some notes. Play strings of eighth and quarter notes.

Final Notes

- Watch the video for ideas.
- Enjoy yourself.

West Street Blues

Level 1: Familiarize by playing chord roots in Left Hand and tune in Right Hand.

Level 2: Pulse the Shells in Left Hand while playing melody in Right Hand. Move to Shells to 5th.

Level 3: Add the 3rds on compression in your Right Hand.

Level 4: Replace melody with C blues scale improvisation in your Right Hand.

Improvisation

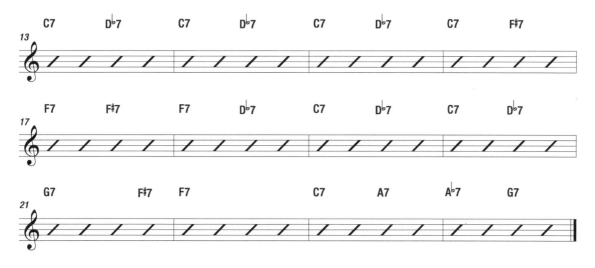

Week 4 Review

3rds

- Can you play 3rds and ♭3rds on compression in the 2516 progression workpiece?
- Can you pedal properly with the shell to the 5th left hand technique?
- Can you play the piece smoothly, pedaling, looking ahead, and positioning your left hand on beat 4?

Stride

- Do you know the 10th stride formation for maj7 chords?
- Can you play the 10th stride for maj7 chords through the master progression?
- Can you play the three maj7 work pieces using the stride?

Patterns

- Do you know how to adjust the patterns for dom7 chords?
- Can you play dom7 patterns through the Master Progression?
- Can you play the dom7 work piece?
- Can you play the 2516 work piece mixing maj7, min7, and dom7 chords?

Diatonic Patterns

- Can you play through the 4 chord progressions and freeform improvise melodies with textures in your right hand?

West Street Blues

- Can you play *West Street Blues* using various left-hand techniques and 3rds on compression in your right hand?
- Can you substitute the C blues scale for the melody in your right hand?

Tunes

- Can you play one of the supplied tunes, or one of your own favorites using:
  1. Shells
  2. Shells to the 5th
  3. Patterns
  4. 3rds on compression

Week 5

What You Will Learn in Week 5

Shells min7♭5 and dim7: The min7♭5 has chord tones of 1 ♭3 ♭5 ♭7, and the dim7 has tones of 1 ♭3 ♭5 ♭♭7. Learn how to adjust and apply shell to the 5th for these chord types.

10th Stride Minor 7th: Learn to adjust the stride for the ♭3rd and ♭7th of the inor 7th chord.

Patterns for min7♭5 and –maj7: The min7♭5 has chord tones of 1 ♭3 ♭5 ♭7 while the –maj7 chords has tones of 1 ♭3 5 7. You will learn how to adjust our 3-note patterns for these chord types.

Diatonics: Learn 2-note patterns for diatonics, and when to use them.

Lazy Lizard Blues: Play this tune with our left-hand techniques and shell to the 5th. Watch out for the ♭3rds in the min7 and min7♭5 chords. Replace the melody with the C blues scale.

Tunes: Choose a tune from one of the six at the end of the book (pages 128–151) or one of your favorites, and apply the techniques you are learning.

Shells Min7♭5 & Dim7 Be Ready
What You Will Learn This Week

The focus of this lesson is finding the 5th for the chord types min7♭5 and dim7. Both of these chords have a ♭5th as the 5th. We will play with shell to the 5th, concentrating and correctly using the 5th or ♭5th in the left hand.

The Video: *Week 5: Min7♭5 and Dim7 Be Ready*

The Exercise

Level 1: Start by getting comfortable with the tune on page 89; play root and melody followed by shell and melody.

Level 2: Then start shell to the 5th and melody, and that is where the fun begins. The min7♭5 and the dim7 will have a ♭5th, while the other chords will have a natural 5th. The shell to the 5th for the min6 is (1, 6) 5.

Level 3: You could even move up to patterns in the left hand, although some of the chords like the dim7 and the min6 will present some difficulty for patterns beyond root–5–octave and root–5–7. Below is an example of the first line of the tune.

Level 4: If you have trouble finding the 5th in the left hand because of all the movement in the right hand, you might simplify the right hand with chord isolation, playing only the note under the chord in the right hand and ignoring the rest.

Play through the piece. Each line is like its own mini-melody. Remember to keep the left hand near the right throughout; this helps to blend the chords between your hands.

Min7♭5 & Dim7 Worksheet
Be Ready!

Level 1: Get comfortable, play melody with root in Left Hand, moving up to Shell in the Left Hand.

Level 2: Play melody with Shell to the 5th in the Left Hand. Watch for ♭5th!

Level 3: Play melody with Patterns in the Left Hand.

Level 4: Simplify the Right Hand if necessary.

Important: Be very careful to flat the 5th on the min7♭5 and dim7 chords.

Min7♭5 & Dim7 Worksheet
"Be Ready"

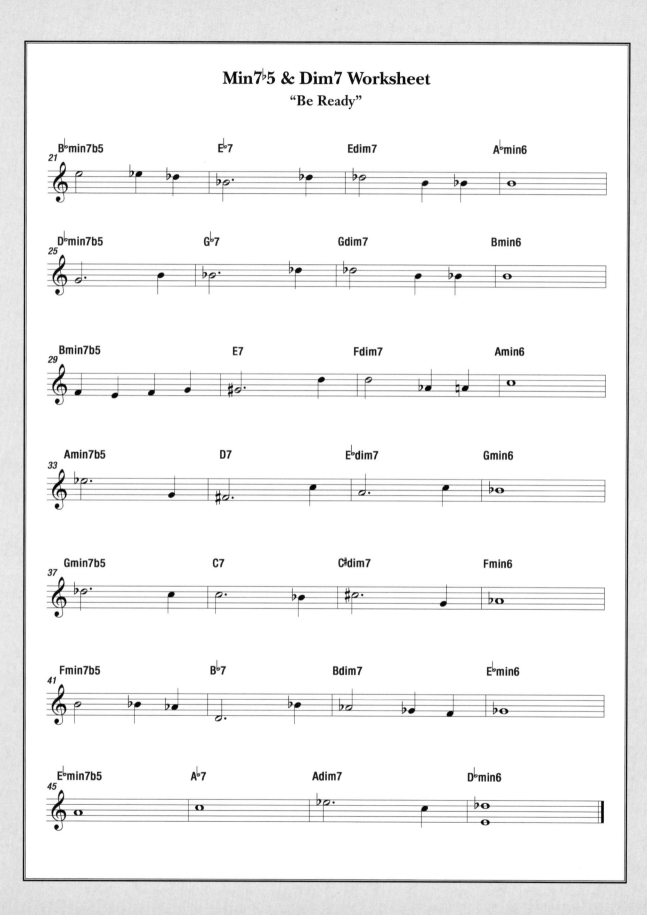

Stride: 10th Stride Formation Min7
What You Will Learn This Week

The stride is a left-hand technique related to the shell to the 5th, in that it outlines the chord and establishes time in your playing. This week, you will learn the min7 formation.

The Video: *Week 5: 10th Stride Min7*

Min7 Stride

The stride is accomplished in your left hand by playing the root (pinky) on beat 1, and then on beat 3 moving your hand up to the 7–10 pair (index–thumb). In this week with the min7, the 7–10 pair is ♭7–♭10.

Pedaling: Pedaling is very important in the stride, to keep the tone ringing as you move your hand from root to 7–10. Remember, it's an opposite effect: let the pedal up as you play the root; then put it back down to hold the root tone as you move your hand up to the 7–10.

Exercises: Level 1

Play the min7 stride through the master progression. Your left hand plays the min7 stride, root to ♭7–♭10 on beats 1 and 3. When you are comfortable, add any chord tone (1 ♭3 5 ♭7) in your right hand on beat 1.

C F B♭ E♭ A♭ D♭ G♭ B E A D G
C E♭ G♭ A C♯ E G B♭ D F A♭ B
C D E F♯ G♯ B♭ C♯ B A G F E♭

Master Progression

You can simplify this level by alternating between two chords, picking different chord tones in your right hand each time.

Level 2

Play the three pieces on the *10th Stride Formation Worksheet* (page 92), stride in your left hand and melody in your right. If you want to simplify to start, play only the first note of the melody for each bar. When comfortable, move up to the full melody in your right hand.

Final Notes
- See what chords you have trouble with, and spend some extra time on them.
- Keep it slow.
- Pedal.
- Works well with shell to the 5th mixed in.

10th Stride Formation Worksheet
(Root—♭7, ♭10 min7)

Level 1: Warm up on Master Progression, stride in Left Hand Root to ♭7 ♭10 on beats (1) and (3), adding any chord tone 1 ♭3 5 ♭7 in Right Hand on beat one when comfortable.

Level 2: Play the Cycle 5, Diminished Progression and Whole Tone Progression "tunes" with Stride in your Left Hand and melody in your Right Hand.

Level 2a: Simplify the Right Hand if necessary, playing only the first note of each bar.

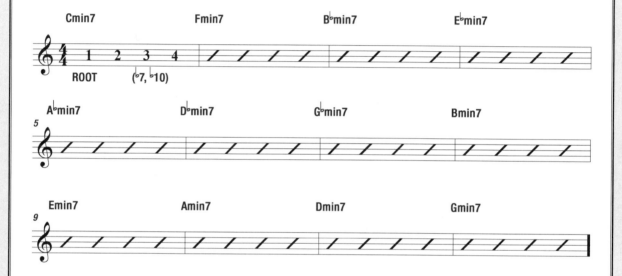

Pedaling

It is a great place to work on effective pedal technique. Isolate the Left Hand alone and remember at the beginning of each Root to be played for the new chord that the pedal comes up to shut off the prior sounds and immediately goes back down to hold the new sounds.

Think Opposite—Root Down—Pedal Up—Right Back Down

C F B♭ E♭ A♭ D♭ G♭ B E A D G

C E♭ G♭ A C♯ E G B♭ D F A♭ B

C D E F♯ G♯ B♭ C♯ B A G F E♭

Master Progression

10th Stride Formation Worksheet

Cycle 5

Diminished Progression

WholeTone Progression

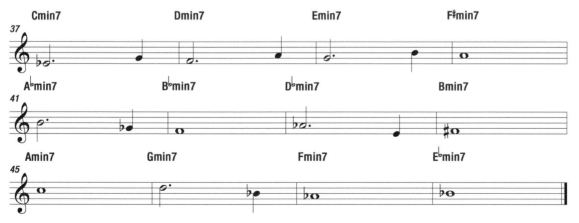

Patterns: Min7♭5 and –Maj7
What You Will Learn This Week

This week has a pair of less frequently found chords, the min7♭5 and the –maj7 (pronounced minor major 7th).

The Video: *Week 5: Min7♭5 Base Patterns minor progression*

min7♭5 and –maj7 Chord Tones

min7♭5	–maj7
1 ♭3 ♭5 ♭7	1 ♭3 5 7

Level 1: Master Progression

First warm up by going through the master progression with min7♭5 and –maj7 patterns in your left hand.

C F B♭ E♭ A♭ D♭ G♭ B E A D G

C E♭ G A C♯ E G B♭ D F A♭ B

C D E F♯ G♯ B♭ C♯ B A G F E♭

Master Progression

For min7♭5, the patterns you should use are:

1–♭5–octave	1–♭5–♭7	1–♭5–♭10	1–♭7–♭10

For –maj7 the pattern you should use is:

1–7–♭10

Level 2: 251 Minor Progression

Once you have loosened up, start on the 251 Minor Progression Worksheet (page 95). This melody with its minor sounds has a nice eerie quality to it. Here's the first line; try it, then move on to the worksheet.

Use the pedal. Fragment where necessary.

Final Notes
- Good example of building patterns from chords not frequently seen.
- Using the ♭10 for the –maj7 works best.

Minor 7♭5 Worksheet
2 5 1 Minor Progression

Level 1: Warm up on Master Progression, playing min7♭5 and -maj7 patterns in Left Hand.

Level 2: Play tune, patterns in Left Hand and melody in Right Hand.

Root ♭5 Octave   Apply Left Hand only for each of the min7♭5 Patterns through all keys, then move onto the –maj7 pattern

Root ♭5 ♭7

Root ♭5 ♭10

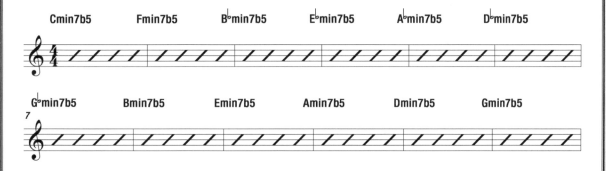

–maj7 (1 7 ♭10)

Important: Be sure to understand that the Chord Tones in a –maj7 chord are Root ♭3rd 5 and 7. The (–) is a symbol for Minor.

Like on the min7♭5 where we had to highlight the ♭5, here we must highlight the 7 and ♭3rd.

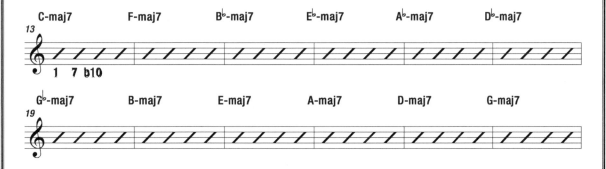

Min7♭5 and –Maj7 Worksheet
251 Minor Progression

Minor Progression—Here we apply our patterns to the Minor Progression. Observe how each key is 4 bars. The first chord is the min7♭5, moving to the dom7, and then resolves itself to the –maj7 chord. I recommend you highlight the 7 and ♭3rd in your pattern to bring out the Minor quality in the progression.

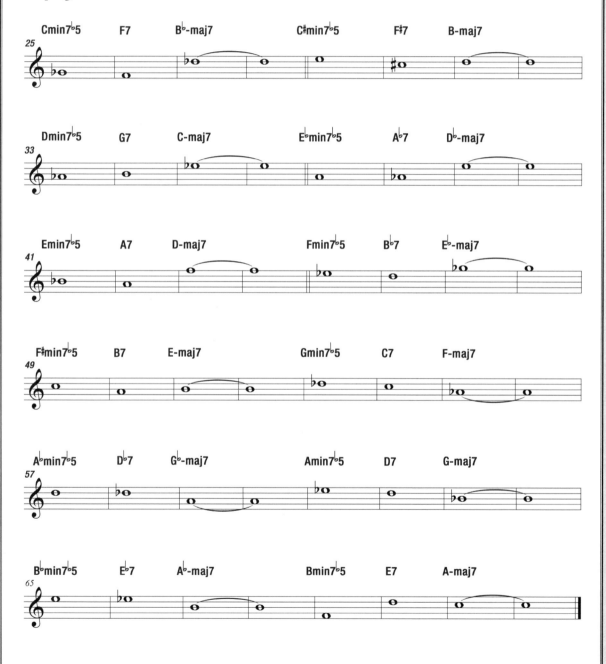

Diatonic Patterns: 2-Note Patterns
What You Will Learn This Week
This week you will work on 2-note diatonic patterns, patterns that take only 2 beats and consist of the first 2 notes of the 3-note patterns that you already know.

The Video: *Week 5: 2 Note Diatonic Patterns on Piece 1*

2 Chords Per Bar
These 2-note patterns are typically applied where you find 2 chords in a bar. You play one 2-note pattern on beats 1 and 2, and another 2-note pattern on beats 3 and 4. Below is an example.

Level 1
Play through the Diatonic 2-Note Patterns Worksheet (page 98), using 2-note patterns when you find 2 chords per bar, and 3-note patterns when you find only 1 chord per bar.

Level 2
When you are comfortable with the patterns in your left hand, start adding white notes under the melody in your right hand. Be careful of void notes as you are adding underneath; you will hear them and make note of it. Again play through the piece.

Level 3
Lastly, make up your own melody, substituting your own white notes for those in the melody. Try to avoid jumping around all over the place; keep your notes close together, even repeating the same note if it sounds good. Any white note will do; however, pay attention to void notes.

Final Note
Always be adjusting your level of application. Make sure you are not going in too deeply and struggling with the piece. If you are, scale back the difficulty until you are comfortable. On the other hand, don't become complacent; always give yourself a reasonable challenge. Find that right balance of challenge vs. comfort.

Diatonic 2-Note Patterns Worksheet
Piece #1

Level 1: Play melody in the Right Hand with Patterns in your Left Hand.

Level 2: Add white notes below the notes in the melody.

Level 3: Substitute your own white notes for the melody.

Lazy Lizard Blues

Here is another fun blues piece that I have put together for you.

The Video: *Week 5:* Lazy Lizard Blues *levels up to 3rds on compression*

Level 1: Familiarize

Play the tune with chord roots in your Left Hand; play them low like a bass line.

Level 2: Pulse, Shells to the 5th

After getting it down, try pulsing the shells in your right hand as you play. Eventually move up to shells to the 5th in the left hand.

Level 3: 3rds on Compression

When comfortable with the tune, try doing 3rds on compression. This tune not only has 3rds, but it has ♭3rds for the min7 chords; watch for those min7 chords and put in the ♭3rd on compression. In the left hand, you can play shells or shells to the 5th, or even the root single-note bass line. Whatever you are comfortable with that allows you to put in the 3rd on compression.

Level 4: C Blues Scale

When done with 3rds on compression, move on to the C blues scale. Choose the left-hand option that you feel comfortable with today. Play the blues scale up and down the keyboard. Rock some notes. Play strings of eighth and quarter notes.

Watch the video for ideas. Enjoy yourself.

Lazy Lizard Blues

Level 1: Familiarize yourself with the tune, melody Right Hand and Roots of chords only in Left Hand.

Level 2: Move up to pulsing Shells or Shell to the 5th in Left Hand.

Level 3: Add the 3rds on compression in your Right Hand.

Level 4: Improvise with the C blues scale.

Improvisation

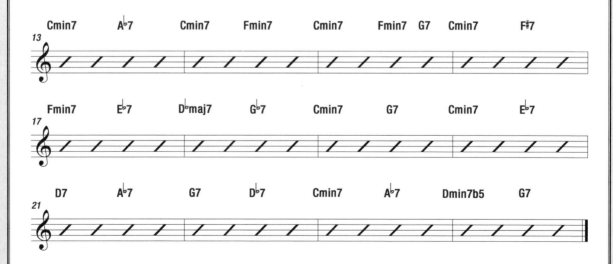

Week 5 Review

Shells
- Can you adjust shells and shells to the 5th for min7♭5 and dim7?
- Can you play the min7♭5 and dim7 work piece using shell to the 5th?

Stride
- Do you know the notes for the 10th stride for min7 chords?
- Can you play the 10th stride work piece smoothly?

Patterns
- Do you know the adjusted chord tones and patterns for min7♭5 and –maj7?
- Can you play the min7♭5 and –maj7 patterns through the master progression?
- Can you smoothly play the 251 minor7♭5 –maj7 work piece?

Diatonic Patterns
- Can you construct 2-note patterns on all our diatonic chords?
- Do you know when to use 2-note patterns?
- Can you play the 2-note pattern work piece?
- Can you create your own melodies using 2-note and 3-note patterns?

Lazy Lizard Blues
- Can you play *Lazy Lizard Blues* using our left-hand techniques?
- Can you play 3rds on compression with the *Lazy Lizard Blues*?
- Can you substitute the C blues scale for the melody?

Tunes
- Can you play one of the supplied tunes, or one of your own favorites using:
  1. Shells
  2. Shells to the 5th
  3. Patterns
  4. Stride
  5. 3rds on compression

Week 6

What You Will Learn in Week 6

3rds Inner Tonal Movement: This week rounds out 3rds with an introduction to inner tonal movement, placing the 3rd in your right hand against the melody in a delayed move. This delay helps fill space and keep time. It is a nice alternative or addition to 3rds on compression.

Shells—More Chord Types: A wrap-up of all chord types, including extended suffix and tone-specific chords, and how to apply shell, shell to the 5th, patterns, and the 3rd when encountering these chord types.

Patterns: In-depth presentation of patterns with dim7 and maj6 chords.

Patterns: Learn 2-note patterns and when to use them.

Stride: The 10th stride on dom7 chords.

Diatonics: Learn how to apply all the techniques we have learned to our diatonic patterns and our diatonic improvisation: shells, shell to the 5th, patterns, stride, 3rds on compression.

1000 Steps Blues: Play with 3rds on compression. Improvise with chord tones and C blues scale.

Tunes: Choose a tune from one of the six at the end of the book (pages 128–151) or one of your favorites, and apply the techniques you are learning.

3rds: Inner Tonal Movement

What You Will Learn This Week

Inner tonal movement is one of my own personal piano skills. I developed this technique many years ago and have been using it and teaching it ever since. The tonal move brings time and interest into your playing. I will introduce it to you here, but bear in mind that inner tonal movement is a big topic, a place where future studies will bring out the full power of inner tonal movement. Here I will show you some examples of the easiest places to insert some inner tonal movement.

The Video: *Week 6: ITM Intro whole to quarter note*

What is an Inner Tonal Movement?

Inner tonal movement is the placement of chord tones and other available tones in the music in situations other than on the compression of the chord. This gives you a chord-tone movement within the measure rather than on the chord. The result is greater depth and harmony in your music, combined with a tonal time keeping.

We will cover chord tones in this book. In future studies you can learn about inner tonal movement of the 9th, and all of the tensions as well.

Shell to the 5th is a Tonal Move

Shell to the 5th is an inner tonal movement occurring in your left hand. You have been using shell to the 5th since week 1, and you should continue using it forever. Notice how it keeps time in your playing.

The 3rd as an Inner Tonal Move

Up to this point you have been using the 3rd on compression to open up chordal harmony between your hands. Now I will show you how to use the 3rd as an inner tonal move, giving you the power to place the 3rd in your melody using the tone as a moving tonal quality (keeping time). Combining this with the 5th, alternating the two tone moves between hands is very effective.

Against the Melody

When applying the inner tonal movement, you must be searching for those "inner" places within the melody to place the 3rd as an added tone. This is much easier when the melody is a half note or greater in value, because it is easier to see the place to insert it. It also works on quarter notes but is more difficult because it is played not on the quarter note, but a half beat later. It can be applied with eighth notes, but it is even more challenging and really not necessary, because the eighth notes are already keeping the time moving.

Examples

Whole Notes: To apply some inner tonal movement with whole notes, see the example below, showing how I place the 3rd in my right hand on beat 2, as well as the 5th in my left hand on beat 3 as part of my shell to the 5th.

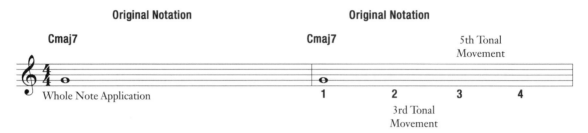

Dotted Half, Half, and Quarter Notes: The example below shows all three techniques: the dotted half, the half, and the quarter note. The dotted-half and half-note examples have the 3rd placed in my right hand on beat 2, and the 5th in my left hand on beat 3 as part of the shell to the 5th. The quarter-note example has the 3rd placed on the "and" of the quarter note, and the 5th on the 3rd beat. This quarter-note treatment is by far the most difficult of the tonal moves. Again, I have penciled in the 3rd notes on the example.

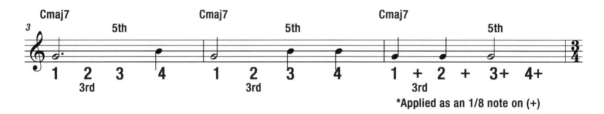

My Wild Irish Rose **Example:** *My Wild Irish Rose*, below, demonstrates how to apply the tonal movement to a tune, a 3/4 tune at that. Notice that the 3rd is on beat 2 in the first three bars and the 5th is on beat 3. Bar 4 is a little tricky, with its two chords and quarter note. You play shells for the chords with no 5th because you have no time for the 5th. You play the 3rd twice, once on beat 2 for the first chord, and once on the "and" of beat 3 for the second chord. Give it a try.

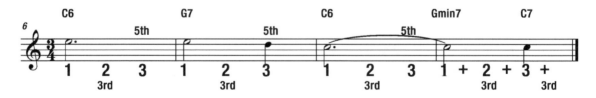

3rds on Compression As Well: You can add even more motion to these last two examples by playing a 3rd on compression on beat 1 in addition to playing the 3rd inner tonal movement on beat 2. I call this 3rd on compression and re-attaching the 3rd as a tonal move. The examples below show what I mean.

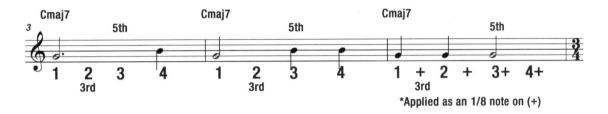

Wild Irish Rose

Final Notes

Watch the video at pianoinstuction.com; this is a complex concept, and watching and hearing me demonstrate it makes it much clearer.

This is an advanced and difficult professional technique. Some of you will be ready to explore inner tonal movement further, while others may wish to stay with 3rds on compression for the upcoming months. If you want to try further, use the tunes as your training ground, or use one of your favorite tunes. Just look for one with a simple melody, not active. A piece with a lot of slow places, whole notes and dotted half notes, giving you time to do the tonal movement. Go through a tune and mark in pencil where you want to have your tonal movement 3rds placed. Then work on the piece until you are comfortable. Remember to fragment and/or simplify to get you up to speed, and to apply the tonal movement smoothly.

There Is More

The compression and re-attach technique is only one of a number of tonal movement techniques for placing the 3rd. If you want to learn more, you can come to our website, and we will have some online lessons for you there. Of course, you could always contact my publisher and express interest for another book.

Shells: More Chord Types
What You Will Learn This Week

Throughout the book, I have demonstrated various chord types and how to use our techniques of 3rd on compression, shells, shell to the 5th, and patterns with each of these chord types. I have created a summary for you on the following pages. If you have done all the various exercises in the past five weeks, this summary should be presenting material that you have already absorbed into your playing skills.

The Video: *Week 6: More Chord Types 3rd comp*

Find the Chord Tones

Even so, the possibility exists that you will find a written chord that doesn't fit into this set of chord types. You play these chords by determining the chord tones and adjusting the formulas for shell, shell to the 5th, patterns, and the 3rd using these chord tones. Here is how to handle most of these cases.

No Suffix: Chords like maj, min, aug, dim have no suffix so you use only the triad formation—1–3–5 of the chord—as chord tones. You build the shell and patterns using only these tones, similarly to the Major and Minor in the table below.

Slash Chords: Chords such as C/E mean that you have a C chord with E in the bass. I like to read it as C *but* E in the bass. For C/E, you should use the bass note twice, an octave apart—e.g., E–E. For the shell to the 5th, you should insert a convenient tone from the chord for the 5th: in the C/E case, the 1 or C works well, giving you E–C–E. The 3rd would be the 3rd of the chord. A pattern is more difficult to come up with a hard-and-fast rule, but either use shell to the 5th instead or build your own pattern starting with the bass note and using chord tones. Pencil it into your piece.

Extended Suffix: Extended-suffix chords are popular; they will typically have an extended suffix using 9ths, 11, ♯11, 13, ♭13. An example would be D7♭9, or F7♯11. What do you do? Right now, you try to determine chord tones that work for you. That usually means using the tones of the chord that you know from the chord type and suffix, and not trying to utilize the extended suffix. In later studies, you can learn techniques that appropriately highlight the extended suffix in your right hand. For now, you should treat the D7♭9 like a D7 or the F7♯11 like a F7.

Tone-Specific: Chords like a ♭9 or ♯9 can be treated as a dom7. Just use the 1–3–5–♭7 tones of the dom7, treating it like a "no-suffix" chord. Future studies will lead you to more advanced solutions on how to adapt using tone specifics in your playing.

Sus4 (1–4–5–♭7): The Sus4 chord is telling you to play the 4 instead of the 3.

min7♭5 (1–♭3–♭5–♭7): Highlight the ♭5 in your left hand to get the full effect of the chord.

dim7 (1–♭3–♭5–♭♭7): Not as common; be prepared to adjust in your left hand.

aug7 (1–3–♯5–♭7): Highlight the ♯5 in your left hand.

maj6 & min6 (1–3–5–6 and 1–♭3–5–6): Highlight the 6 in your shell.

Summary: The following page has a Chord Tone Summary Sheet of all the chord types we have covered in this book, their chord tones, and how to adjust our techniques for these chords. This has been covered, but I wanted to summarize it for you.

Exercises

Level 1: Chord Tones Go through the summary sheet, using the key of C, and find all the adjusted chord tones in your left hand for all the chord types. Start with C Major, C Minor, Cmaj7. Work your way down the entire sheet and give yourself some practice on how to adjust the chord tones.

Level 2: More Chord Types Workpiece Play through the More Chord Types Worksheet (page 110), shell to the 5th in your left hand and 3rd on compression in your right hand. This will be a challenge. You will have to think about every chord, and you probably won't be able to do it smoothly. I primarily want you to get a feel of the process of adjusting your left-hand and right-hand techniques. Each bar will have you playing all the chord tones for the chord. All the chord types will be presented within the piece. In real life, you probably won't run up against anything this difficult. It is more likely that you will infrequently run across a few tough chords, and you should know how to adjust and pencil it in if necessary.

Watch the Video: Watch the video, where I play the workpiece and talk you through all the adjustments and highlights of each chord type.

Chord Tone Summary Sheet

Level 1: Using the key of C, go through this worksheet and find all the adjusted chord tones and apply them to the Shell, Shell to the 5th, and Patterns.

Chord Type	Chord Tones				3rd	Shell	Shell to 5th	Pattern
	1	3	5	7				
Major	1	3	5		3	1–octave 1–5	(1, octave)–5	1–5–octave 1–5–10
Minor	1	♭3	5		♭3	1–octave 1–5	(1, octave)–5	1–5–octave 1–5–♭10
Diminished	1	♭3	♭5		♭3	1–octave 1–b5	(1, octave)–b5	1–b5–octave 1–b5–b10
Augmented	1	3	♯5		3	1–octave 1–♯5	(1, octave)–♯5	1–♯5–octave 1–♯5–10
maj7	1	3	5	7	3	1–7	(1, 7)–5	1–5–octave 1–5–7 1–5–10 1–7–10
dom7	1	3	5	♭7	3	1–♭7	(1, ♭7)–5	1–5–octave 1–5–♭7 1–5–10 1–♭7–10
min7	1	♭3	5	♭7	b3	1–♭7	(1, ♭7)–5	1–5–octave 1–5–♭7 1–5–♭10 1–♭7–♭10
min7♭5	1	♭3	♭5	♭7	♭3	1–♭7	(1, ♭7)–♭5	1–♭5–octave 1–♭5–♭7 1–♭5–♭10 1–♭7–♭10
dim7	1	♭3	♭5	♭♭7	♭3	1–♭♭7	(1, ♭♭7)–♭5	1–♭5–octave 1–♭5–♭♭7 1–♭5–♭10 1–♭♭7–♭10

maj6	1	3	5	6	3	1–6	(1, 6)–5	1–5–octave 1–5–6 1–5–10 1–6–10
min6	1	♭3	5	6	♭3	1–6	(1, 6)–5	1–5–octave 1–5–6 1–5–♭10 1–6–♭10
aug7	1	3	♯5	♭7	3	1–♭7	(1, ♭7)–♯5	1–♯5–octave 1–♯5–♭7 1–♯5–10 1–♭7–10
sus4	1	4	5	7	4	1–7	(1, 7)–5	1–5–octave 1–5–7 1–5–11 1–7–11
Slash Chord e.g. C/E chord/bass	Bass 1 3 5 of chord				3	Bass–octave e.g. E E	Bass (1 or 3 or 5) bass octave e.g. (E, E)–1	Make your own from bass 1 3 5
Extended suffix e.g. Dmin7♭9, C7♯11	Tones of chord e.g. 1 3 5 ♭7				3	From chord	From chord	From chord
Tone Specific ♭9 ♯9	1 3 5 of chord				3	1–octave	(1, octave)–5	1–5–octave 1–5–10

Different publications will use different "short-hand" notations for chord types. Here are the ones that you will come across most often.

Major7	Minor7	Dominant7	Augmented7	Major6	Minor6	Diminished7
maj7	min7	dom7	aug7	maj6	min6	dim7
M7	m7	7	+7	M6	m6	°7
Δ7	-7			6	-6	

Final Notes

Watch the video at www.pianoinstruction.com and see how I adjust for all the chords in the workpiece.

3rds on Compression Worksheet
More Chord Types

Level 2: Play the Worksheet with Shells to the 5th in the Left Hand, and melody with the 3rds applied on compression in the Right Hand.

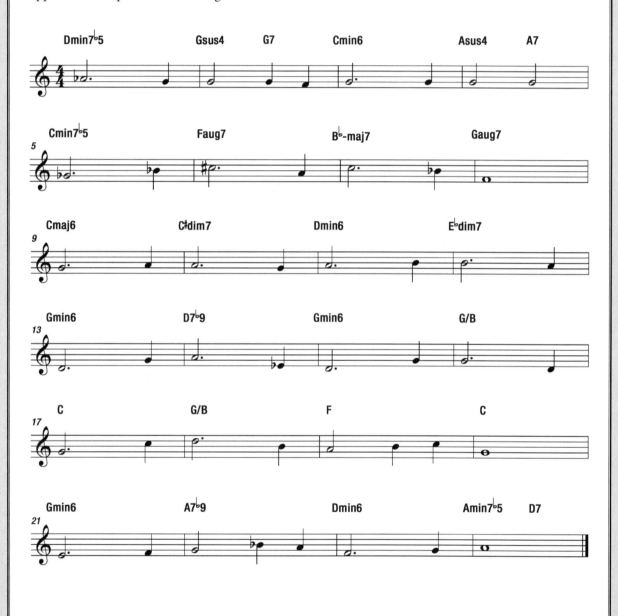

Stride: 10th Stride Formation Dom7
What You Will Learn This Week

This week presents the dom7 stride. Examples of its use in our six supplied tunes is demonstrated.

The Video: *Week 6: 10th Stride Dom7 and Tune Samples*

Dom7 Stride

The stride is a left-hand technique related to the shell to the 5th in that it outlines the chord and establishes time in your playing. The stride is accomplished in your left hand by playing the root (pinky) on beat 1, and then on beat 3 moving your hand up to the 7–10 pair (index–thumb). In this week with the dom7, the 7–10 pair is ♭7–10. Example below.

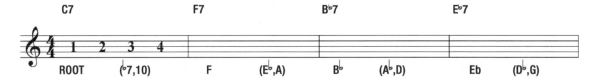

Pedaling: Pedaling is very important in the stride, to keep the tone ringing as you move your hand from root to 7–10. Remember it's an opposite effect. Let the pedal up as you play the root. Then immediately put it back down to hold the root tone and the 7–10.

Exercises: dom7

Play the dom7 stride through the master progression. Your left hand plays the dom7 stride, root to ♭7–10 on beats 1 and 3. When you are comfortable, add any chord tone (1 3 5 ♭7) in your right hand on beat 1.

C F B♭ E♭ A♭ D♭ G♭ B E A D G

C E♭ G♭ A C♯ E G B♭ D F A♭ B

C D E F♯ G♯ B♭ C♯ B A G F E♭

Master Progression

You can simplify this level by alternating between two chords, picking different chord tones in your right hand each time.

Other Chord Types

You can build stride patterns for other chord types by knowing the tones of the chord. Here are the stride formations for other common chord types.

maj6	1 (6 10)	min6	1 (6 ♭10)
dim7	1 (♭♭7 ♭10)	min7♭5	1 (♭7 ♭10)
aug7	1 (♭7 10)	No suffix (e.g. C)	1 (5 10)
Csus4	1 (♭7 11(4th))		

Play patterns with these chord types through the master progression.

Our 6 Tunes

I've included samples of our 6 tunes (pages 114–116). I have marked the samples with Xs to indicate when to play the 7–10 of the stride. I play these tunes at the end of the video for this lesson.

The Video: *Week 6: 10th Stride Dom7 and Tune Samples*

Indian Summer: Play the stride on beats 1 and 3. For bars containing 2 chords, play shells.

After You've Gone: Play the stride on beats 1 and 3. For bars containing 2 chords, play shells.

My Wild Irish Rose: My Wild Irish Rose is written in 3/4 time, meaning 3 beats per measure. Play the stride on beats 1 and 2.

Indiana: Play the stride on beats 1 and 3. For bars containing 2 chords, play shells.

Happy Birthday: Happy Birthday has 2 chords per bar throughout, so you should play the stride for each chord. Play first chord on beats 1 and 2 and second chord on beats 3 and 4.

Shenandoah: Shenandoah has 2 chords per bar throughout, so you should play the stride for each chord. Play first chord on beats 1 and 2 and second chord on beats 3 and 4. This is a workout. Take it a line at a time.

Final Notes

- Pedal.
- Stride works well with shell to the 5th mixed in. Any time you have trouble playing the stride with some of the chords that you don't see very often, substitute the shell to the 5th, as it will provide the necessary time-keeping and tonal sound.
- Try the stride on your own favorites.

10th Stride Formation Worksheet
Root—♭7, 10 (Dom7)

dom7 Chord—We now put our focus on the dom7 Chord. Here we have the ♭7 and the 10, which will define this chord quality. The dom7 Chord is one of the commonly seen chord types and will now have us completing the maj7 and min7 and now dom7.

How to Build Your Stride—It is important to understand the formula in how to build a chord. As you can see, the Stride has the Root, then the top part of the Shell and the 3rd of that chord played high to give us the 10th span in your Left Hand. Other chord types are listed below.

Left Hand—Root to ♭7, 10 on beats (1) and (3).
Right Hand—Play any Chord Tone 1, ♭3, 5, or ♭7 and each new chord choose the next Chord Tone to be close.

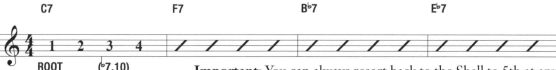

Important: You can always resort back to the Shell to 5th at any time you wish as the Stride and Shell to 5th share the same chord defining quality and time keeping function.

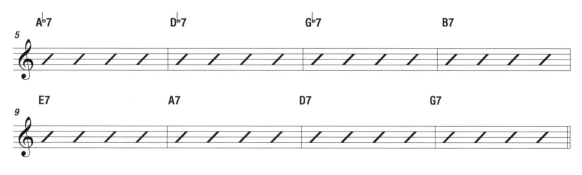

Major 6th—Root (6, 10)   Minor7♭5—Root (♭7, ♭10)
Minor 6th—Root (6, ♭10)   Augmented7—Root (♭7, 10)
Diminished7—Root (♭♭7, ♭10)

*Note that both these chord types have an altered 5th which will not be affected by the 10 Stride Formation.

C F B♭ E♭ A♭ D♭ G♭ B E A D G
C E♭ G♭ A C♯ E G B♭ D F A♭ B
C D E F♯ G♯ B♭ C♯ B A G F E♭

Master Progression

10th Stride Formation Worksheet
Tune Samples

Indian Summer

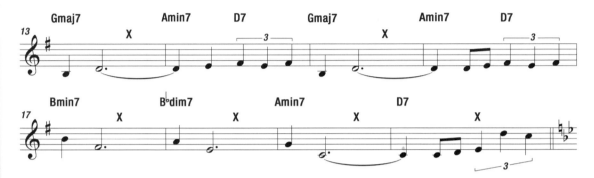

After You've Gone

My Wild Irish Rose

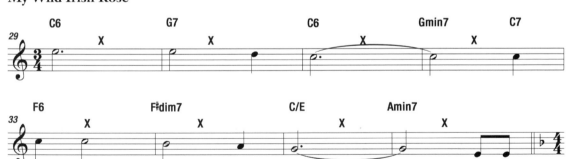

(X) will indicate where you will be placing the (7, 10) part of the 10th Stride Formation.

Important: Observe how the Stride Formation in our tune samples is mostly on beats 1 and 3, and not used on 2 chords per bar. (Just use Shells here.) We do, however, have a few exceptions here. In the 3/4 piece, we had (7, 10) come on beat 2, and 2 of the piece we had established the time on each beat for 2 chords per bar.

10th Stride Formation Worksheet
Tune Samples

Indiana

Happy Birthday

Shenandoah

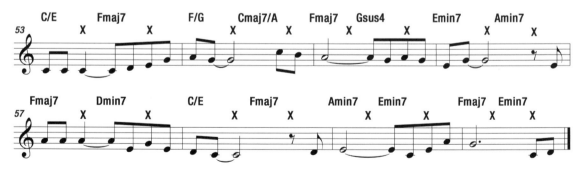

Patterns: Diminished 7 and Major 6

What You Will Learn This Week

This week you will be shown dim7 base patterns and maj6 base patterns. By the end of this lesson, you will have been presented patterns for all the chord types.

The Video: *Week 6: Base Patterns Dim7 and Maj6 application*

More Flat Tones and a 6th

The dim7 and the maj6 have a different set of flat tones. The dim7 is $1\ ^\flat3\ ^\flat5\ ^{\flat\flat}7$, and the maj6 is 1 3 5 6.

Our typical patterns get modified to fit these chord types as outlined below.

	1–5–octave	1–5–7	1–5–10	1–7–10
dim7 adjustment	$1–^\flat5$–octave	$1–^\flat5–^\flat7$	$1–^\flat5–^\flat10$	$1–^{\flat\flat}7–^\flat10$
maj6 adjustment	1–5–octave	1–5–6	1–5–10	1–6–10

Play through the Patterns Worksheet (page 117) using the patterns in your left hand and the melody in your right.

Level 1
1–5–octave and melody

Level 2
1–5–7 and melody

Level 3
1–5–10 and melody

Level 4
1–7–10 and melody

Level 5
Change pattern every line

If you find that you are having difficulty with any chord, repeat it a few times to get comfortable.

Patterns Worksheet
The "Diminished 7 Chord" & "Maj6"

Base Patterns now focus on the diminished7 and maj6 chord types. This progression provides a musical platform for you to see in actual application. Master each of the Base Patterns.

Level 1: Stride (1-5-octave) and melody.
Level 2: Stride (1-5-7) and melody.
Level 3: Stride (1-5-10) and melody.
Level 4: Stride (1-7-10) and melody.
Level 5: Change Stride pattern with every line.

Important: Modify the shape to fit the dim7 and maj6 chord types.

Patterns Worksheet
Dim7 & Maj6 Application

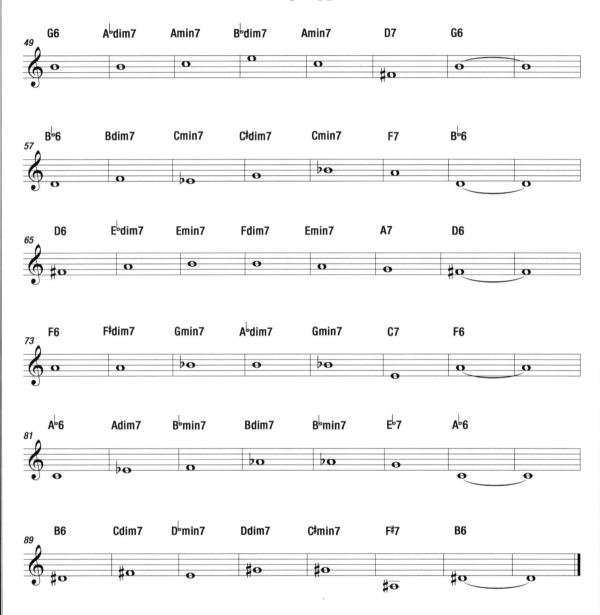

Patterns: 2-Note Patterns
What You Will Learn This Week
This week you will learn about 2-note patterns and when to apply them.

The Video: *Week 6: 2 note patterns*

2 Chords Per Measure
Very often in your playing, you will come across situations with 2 chords in a measure. This gives you only 2 beats per chord, and our 3-note patterns have been functioning in 3 beats. You solve this by modifying the patterns to use only 2 beats as shown below.

1–octave	1–5	1–7	1–10

2–Note Patterns

In doing this, you should try to choose a pattern that contains the defining note of the chord. For example, a min7♭5 should use the 1–♭5, and a maj6 should use a 1–6.

Level 1: Exercise
Play through the 2-Note Pattern Worksheet (page 120), using 2-note patterns where you have 2 chords per bar, and 3-note patterns where you have 1 chord per bar. Watch out for the bars with ties; you will be starting the second pattern without playing a note in your right hand.

Final Notes
- Shell to the 5th can be an alternative to the 2-note pattern.
- Use 2-note patterns with 2 chords per bar.
- Use 3-note patterns with 1 chord per bar.

The 2-Note Pattern Worksheet

2-Note Pattern—It is very important to fully understand how to modify our 3-Note Base Pattern and create the 2-Note Pattern. The 3-Note Pattern is typically playing 3 quarter notes and where you usually see this come into play first is on those measures where you have 2 chords in a 4/4 bar. Each chord must receive 2 beats. Obviously the 3-Note Pattern will be adjusted here to fit. Typically you can look at this as play the Root and any of the other notes from the pattern. Often, a specific chord type like min7♭5 the ♭5 is recommended to put in the pattern unless at times you see it in the melody where that tone is heard.

Shell to 5th is an option instead of a modification of the pattern. You can always refer back to this because remember all we are doing here is keeping the time established and the Shell to the 5th will accomplish that.

2-Note Pattern Options:

Root—Octave   Root—5th   Root—7th   Root—10

Level 1: Play workpiece with 2 note patterns in bars with 2 chords, and 3 note patterns in bars with 1 chord.

Diatonic: Chords
What You Will Learn This Week
This week shows you how to apply all the skills learned in the last six weeks to our diatonic patterns, letting you do diatonic improvisation with all of your skills.

The Video: *Week 6: Diatonics merge skills*

Combine Your Skills
During the past 5 weeks, Diatonics have been used as 7 simple 3-note patterns that can be used with all white keys (the key of C). This has provided an uncomplicated platform for you to start moving your hands all over the keyboard, exploring many right-hand options, playing whatever you want.

    This week we merge the diatonic patterns with all the other skills you have learned: shells, shell to the 5th, patterns, and stride. In doing this, you get to use all the techniques learned in the past 5 weeks and combine them with the improvisation techniques offered by the diatonics.

Notes to Play
In the Diatonic Chords Worksheet (page 122), I have supplied the notes to use for the 7 diatonic chords. Of course, you probably could figure them out yourself based on all the exercises that you have done in the past 5 weeks; after all, they are just chords like the ones you have seen for 5 weeks. I just saved you the trouble by doing it myself.

Level 1: Warm Up
Play through these chords with all the different techniques to get warmed up, starting with diatonic patterns and working through shells, shells to the 5th, patterns, and stride.

Level 2: The Tune
The second page of worksheets contains a short tune. Play through it with the different techniques.

Level 3: Improvisation
The second page of worksheets contains an improvisation piece. Play through it with different left-hand techniques and play your own improvisational right hand.

Final Notes
- Have some fun.
- Watch the video at pianoinstruction.com to hear how I do it.

Diatonic Chords Worksheet
Merge Your Applications

Level 1: Warm up by playing all of the techniques with all the chords.

Diatonic Chords and Patterns

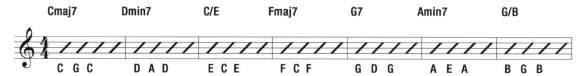

Cmaj7	Dmin7	C/E	Fmaj7	G7	Amin7	G/B
C G C	D A D	E C E	F C F	G D G	A E A	B G B

Shells and Shell to 5th

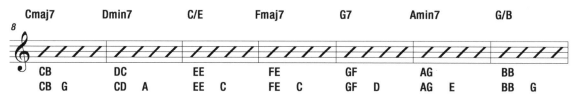

Cmaj7	Dmin7	C/E	Fmaj7	G7	Amin7	G/B
CB	DC	EE	FE	GF	AG	BB
CB G	CD A	EE C	FE C	GF D	AG E	BB G

Octave Patterns—Shells and Diatonic Pattern
The Shells fall within the Octave Pattern Range

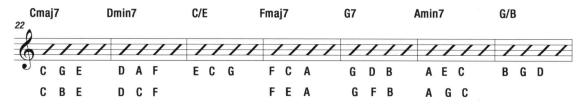

Cmaj7	Dmin7	C/E	Fmaj7	G7	Amin7	G/B
C G B	D A C	*E C E	F C E	G D F	A E G	*B G B

*Two of the Octave Patterns is the Diatonic Pattern

10th Patterns

Cmaj7	Dmin7	C/E	Fmaj7	G7	Amin7	G/B
C G E	D A F	E C G	F C A	G D B	A E C	B G D
C B E	D C F		F E A	G F B	A G C	

Base Stride

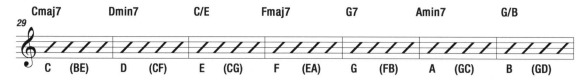

Cmaj7	Dmin7	C/E	Fmaj7	G7	Amin7	G/B
C (BE)	D (CF)	E (CG)	F (EA)	G (FB)	A (GC)	B (GD)

Diatonic Chords—Applications
Diatonic–Shell–Patterns–Stride

Level 2: Playing through this tune with all the techniques.

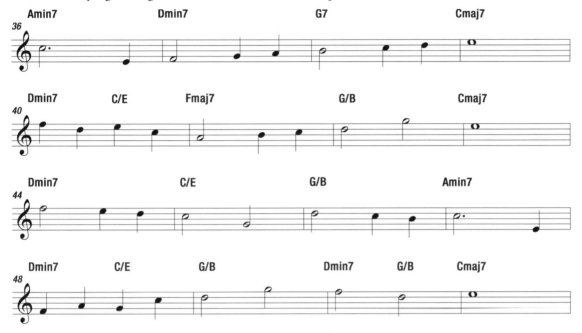

Improvisation
Level 3: 1 chord tone per chord.

Level 3b: Dotted half to quarter.

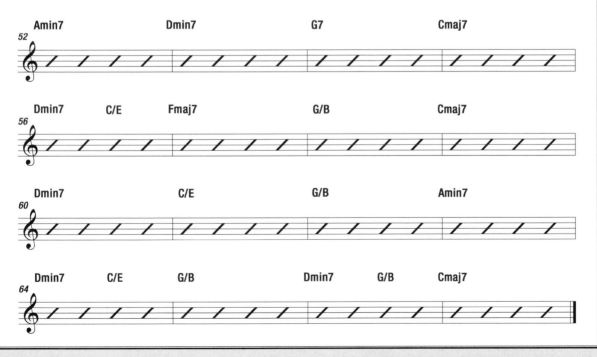

1000 Steps Blues **Improvisation**

1000 Steps Blues is another piece that I have written. It is unusual in that it is a very bluesy tune, but it doesn't follow a traditional blues chord progression. This means that in playing, sometimes you can get it sounding a little more like a ballad than a blues tune. Also, when improvising, you can't really use the C blues scale on the first two lines; you need to use chord tones for the improvisation. The third line works well with the C blues scale.

The Video: *Week 6: 1000 Step Blues*

Play the tune and work your way through various levels.

Level 1

Single-note bass lines in the left hand composed of the roots of the chords. Melody in the right hand. Fragment to get the melody under control.

Level 2

Shells and melody.

Level 3

Shells to the 5th and melody. On the bars containing 2 chords, you could be relaxed and play just shells, or you could be aggressive and play shell to the 5th for the 1st chord on beats 1 and 2, and then shell to the 5th for the second chord on beats 3 and 4.

Level 4

Shells to the 5th with 3rds on compression in the right hand. Be relaxed and play shells for the bars with 2 chords and shells to the 5th for the bars with 1 chord.

Level 5 Improvisation

For the first 2 lines, improvise with chord tones. The third line is appropriate for the C blues scale improvisation.

Watch the video at pianoinstruction.com.

1000 Steps Blues

Level 1: Single Note Bass Line (Roots of Chord) and melody.

Level 2: Left Hand Shells and melody in the Right Hand.

Level 3: Left Hands Shells to 5th and melody in Right Hand

Level 4: Add 3rds on compression

Level 5: Improvise first two lines with chord tones and C Blues Scale for the 3rd line.

Improvisation

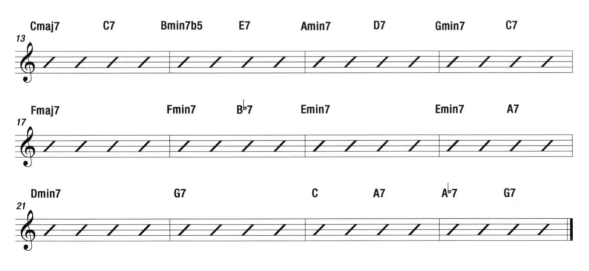

Week 6 Review

Shells

- Are you confident that you can take any chord you run across and figure out the notes to play for the shell, shell to the 5th, patterns, stride, 3rd on compression, and inner tonal movement?

3rds: Inner Tonal Movement

- Do you know what two tones are used for inner tonal movement, one in your left hand and one in your right hand?
- Can you identify "inner" places in melodies to apply the 3rd as an inner tonal movement?
- Do you know where to apply the 3rd as an inner tonal movement with whole notes?
- Do you know where to apply the 3rd as an inner tonal movement with dotted half notes?
- Do you know where to apply the 3rd as an inner tonal movement with half notes?
- Do you know where to apply the 3rd as an inner tonal movement with quarter notes?
- Do you know how to apply the 3rd on compression and re-attach as an inner tonal movement?
- Have you watched the video?

Stride

- Do you know the adjusted chord tones for the 10th stride for dom7 chords?
- Can you play the 10th stride work piece smoothly?

Patterns

- Do you know the adjusted chord tones and patterns for dim7 and maj6?
- Can you play the dim7 and maj6 patterns through the master progression?
- Can you smoothly play the dim7 and maj6 work piece?
- Do you know the 4 options for 2-note patterns?
- Do you know where to apply 2-note patterns?
- Can you smoothly play the 2-note pattern workpiece?

Diatonic Patterns

- Can you play the diatonic chords as a shell, shell to the 5th, pattern, stride?
- Can you play the supplied tune using our 4 left-hand techniques?
- Can you create your own melodies with improvisation work piece using our 4 left-hand techniques?

1000 Steps Blues

- Can you play *1000 Steps Blues* using our left-hand techniques?
- Can you play 3rds on compression with the *1000 Steps Blues*?
- Can you substitute the C blues scale for the melody where appropriate and do a little chord-tone improvisation elsewhere?

Tunes

I have supplied six tunes for you to play using your new skills. You can play these in any order you like, although I have arranged them in order of difficulty. You should augment these tunes with your own favorites. There are many good, inexpensive fake books available in a number of different genres. Just look around on the Internet, and you will find what you want.

The tunes supplied are each played with four different styles: shells, shells to the 5th, patterns, and 3rds on compression. You won't be able to play every style in Week 1; here is my suggested progression.

Week 1: Shells

Week 2: Shells or shells to the 5th

Week 3: Shells or shells to the 5th or patterns

Week 4 or 5: 3rds on compression, typically with shells to the 5th in the left hand.

Free Videos: Watch the videos for these tunes at www.pianoinstruction.com. You will gain insight on how to play the various options, the sound and tempo of the tune, and how to plan for every little issue that will come your way. There are 4 videos for each tune.

Indian Summer

Choose a playing option that you are comfortable with today.

Videos

Indian Summer: *Indian Summer with shells and melody*

Indian Summer: *Indian Summer with shell to the 5th and melody*

Indian Summer: *Indian Summer with base patterns applied*

Indian Summer: *Indian Summer with 3rds on compression*

Watch the videos on www.pianoinstruction.com. You will gain insight on how to play the various options, the sound and tempo of the tune, and how to plan for every little issue that will come your way. Reference the *Indian Summer* score.

Shells

Play the 1–7 shells in your left hand and the melody in your right hand.

Key Signature: The key signature is the key of G; all Fs will be sharp unless otherwise noted by a natural sign.

Ties: There are ties throughout this piece. A tie will connect 2 or more notes on the same line, adding up their total note value. The tie starting in the first bar adds up to 4 beats, starting on the 2nd beat of the first bar and continuing through the first beat of the second bar. In this case you will be playing the Amin7 at the start of the second bar while adding nothing in the right hand until beat 2.

Triplets: There are quarter-note triplets throughout that have you playing 3 notes in 2 beats. This is a very complicated rhythm, and I teach the technical side of this in my more advanced studies. Right now, don't worry about counting them. The best approach is to watch the video and hear how they sound.

Shells to the 5th

A Mainstay: Shells to the 5th is a very important skill; it is a mainstay of your playing that you will use all the time. Shells to the 5th can be applied in many ways. Each tune will have its own time signature and chord layout. In time you will develop what you like to put forth in your playing. In this case, with 4/4 timing, play the 5th on beats 1 and 3. On measures with 2 chords, try playing just the shell.

Pedaling: Remember your pedaling: up and then down at the start of each chord. This allows you to hear all three tones of the chord together, while giving you an opportunity to reposition, setting up your left hand after playing the 5th on beat 3. An entire beat+ to get in position for the next chord. A good rule is to be in position, ready to play the next shell when you are on beat 4 – one full beat before the next chord.

2 Chords Per Bar: On bars with 2 chords, as in bar 2, revert to playing only the shell for each chord.

Flat 5th: On bars 6, 9, and 22 you will find either a dim7 or a min7♭5 chord. Both of these chords have a flat 5th, something that we cover in Week 5. If you are here earlier, you have two options. You can play the flat 5th, which is one note down from the natural 5th, or you can play just the shell for these bars, omitting the 5th.

Base Patterns

4 Patterns: You have four patterns to choose from: 1–5–octave, 1–5–7, 1–5–10, and 1–7–10. Start with 1–5–octave and work your way through the others as you are comfortable. For the measures with two chords, play a 2-note pattern for each chord; use the 1-10 or 1-♭10. The patterns using only the 10th require the 3rd and the ♭3rd, so make sure you are comfortable with these chord tones before trying the 10th patterns, probably in Week 4 or Week 5.

It is a wonderful feeling when you can blend skills together with an element of finesse. Having all of these options makes it fun to seamlessly connect the various styles into one musical package.

2 Chords per Bar: There are quite a few instances of 2 chords per bar in this piece, and your pattern won't fit. You have options to choose from:
1. Play the 1, 7 Shell for each chord.
2. Invent a 2-note pattern, either the 1–5, the 1–7, or the 1–octave. Play the 2-note pattern for each chord in the bar.
3. Play shell to the 5th on beats 1 and 2, and another shell to the 5th on beats 3 and 4.

Vary Your Options: You can vary your left-hand options throughout the piece, moving from one pattern to another, throwing in shells to the 5th for a while. Sometimes you do this because you need to solve a problem, like 2 chords per bar, or you don't know how to find a ♭3rd or ♭5th. Sometimes you do this just because you want to.

Chord Isolation: If you are having difficulty playing the left-hand patterns smoothly, try chord isolation at the start. With chord isolation, you ignore most of the melody in the right hand and instead play only the note under the chord. This allows you to concentrate more on your patterns. As you get comfortable, you can move up to the full melody.

3rds on Compression

My Favorite Combination: This option shows my favorite style, shell to the 5th in my left hand and 3rds on compression in my right hand. Make sure you are good with shells to the 5th and melody before moving up to this style. I start showing you 3rds on compression in Week 2; it is best to wait at least until then, if not Weeks 3 or 4.

Ties: The ties that go from one bar to the next need a solution. Do you play the 3rd on the compression of the chord, or do you play it on the compression of the first note in the bar, which is on beat 2? The answer is that you play the 3rd on the compression of the chord, below the tie note. There is no need to re-compress the tie note; you should be holding that down already.

Indian Summer

After You've Gone

Choose a playing option that you are comfortable with today.

Videos

After You've Gone: After You've Gone with shells and melody

After You've Gone: After You've Gone with shell to the 5th and melody

After You've Gone: After You've Gone with base patterns applied

After You've Gone: After You've Gone with 3rds on compression

Watch the videos on www.pianoinstruction.com. You will gain insight on how to play the various options, the sound and tempo of the tune, and how to plan for every little issue that will come your way.

Shells

Play the 1–7 shells in your left hand and the melody in your right hand.

Key signature: The key signature is the key of $B^\flat$; all Bs and Es will be flat unless otherwise noted by a natural sign.

Slash Chords: There are a few slash chords in this piece, and I don't cover this until Week 3. If you are here earlier, play the note to the right of the slash with your pinky and thumb, an octave apart to create the shell. For example, for C/E play two Es an octave apart.

Chords with no suffix: If you run across a chord like a $B^\flat$ in the slash chord, you can try a $B^\flat$maj7 or $B^\flat$7 or a $B^\flat$6. Try them until you find one that sounds good against the melody and pencil it in. If none seem to work, try playing octaves.

Fragment: Always think about fragmenting at any troublesome areas you run into, and repeat 2 to 4 bars until you are comfortable.

Shell to the 5th

A Mainstay: Shell to the 5th is a very important skill; it is a mainstay of your playing that you will use all the time. Inserting the 5th gives you a steady flow of time. Play the shell in your left hand on beat 1 and the 5th on beat 3, along with the melody in your right hand. When you come across 2 chords in a measure, use only the shell, or see *Another Option* below.

Another Option: You could also take this piece and play the shell to the 5th on beats 1 and 2, and then repeat it on beats 3 and 4. Slow the melody down to give yourself time to do the left-hand work. In this piece, bar 1 would have E♭maj7 on beats 1 and 2, and it would be repeated on beats 3 and 4. Bar 2 would have E♭min7 on beats 1 and 2, and A♭7 on beats 3 and 4.

Pedaling: Remember your pedaling, up and down at the start of each chord. This allows you to carry the left hand selection while giving you an opportunity to reposition your left hand.

Chord Isolation: The perfect breakdown! If you are having difficulty playing the left hand smoothly, try chord isolation at the start. With chord isolation, you ignore most of the melody in the right hand and instead play only the note under the chord. This allows you to concentrate more on your left hand. As you get comfortable, you can move up to the full melody.

Base Patterns

4 Patterns: You have four patterns to choose from, 1–5–octave, 1–5–7, 1–5–10, and 1–7–10. Start with 1–5–octave and work your way up as you are comfortable. The patterns using the 10th require the 3rd and the ♭3rd, so make sure you are comfortable with these chord tones before trying 10th patterns, probably Week 4 or Week 5.

Not the Best Tune for Patterns: Although this is not the best tune for patterns, you should give it a try. Many of the bars have more than 1 chord, and on these you need to fall back to shell to the 5th. But the ones that will fit the patterns sound very nice.

Another Option: As in the shell to the 5th option, the base patterns can be played by slowing the melody down and playing the pattern twice per bar. In bar 1 you play the E♭maj7 twice, counting "1 and 2 and" for the first time and "3 and 4 and" for the second time. Bar 2 would have you play an E♭min7 followed by an Amin7 pattern.

Chord Isolation: If you are having difficulty playing the left-hand patterns smoothly, try chord isolation at the start. With chord isolation, you ignore most of the melody in the right hand and instead play only the note under the chord. This allows you to concentrate more on your patterns. As you get comfortable, you can move up to the full melody.

3rds on Compression

My Favorite Combination: This option shows my favorite style, shell to the 5th in my left hand and 3rds on compression in my right hand. Make sure you are good with shells to the 5th and melody before moving up to this style. I start showing you 3rds on compression in Week 2; it is best to wait at least until then, if not Week 3 or 4.

Keep it Slow: Your right hand has so much to do that keeping the pace slow makes the tune much more relaxed.

2 Chords per Bar: Try either a shell (easy) or shell to the 5th on beats 1 and 2 and another on beats 3 and 4 (hard). Remember to play a 3rd at the compression of each of the chords.

Chord Isolation: You can do chord isolation if you are having problems here. With chord isolation, you ignore most of the melody in the right hand and instead play only the note under the chord. In this case, however, you need to add the 3rd below the melody note as well.

After You've Gone

My Wild Irish Rose

Choose a playing option that you are comfortable with today.

Videos

My Wild Irish Rose: My Wild Irish Rose with shells and melody

My Wild Irish Rose: My Wild Irish Rose with shell to the 5th and melody

My Wild Irish Rose: My Wild Irish Rose with base patterns applied

My Wild Irish Rose: My Wild Irish Rose with 3rds on compression

Watch the videos on www.pianoinstruction.com. You will gain insight on how to play the various options, the sound and tempo of the tune, and how to plan for every little issue that will come your way.

Shells

Play the 1–7 shells in your left hand and the melody in your right hand.

Key Signature: The key signature is the key of C, no flats or sharps. However, in the middle of the second page it changes to the key of F, where all Bs are flat.

Time Signature: This piece is in 3/4 time, 3 beats per measure. This doesn't affect you too much when playing shells, but it has an impact later when playing shell to the 5th.

The Form: The form of this tune is important to note. Observe the repeat signs and the 1st and 2nd endings.

Slash Chords and Others: There are a few slash chords in this piece, and I don't cover this until Week 3. If you are here earlier, play the note to the right of the slash with your pinky and thumb, an octave apart to create the shell. For example, for C/E, play two Es an octave apart.

For chords with no suffix, like C or F, play the 1–5 or 1–octave to create the shell.

Fragment: Always think about fragmenting at some troublesome area, and repeat 2 to 4 bars until you are comfortable.

Shells to the 5th

A Mainstay: Shell to the 5th is a very important skill; it is a mainstay of your playing that you will use all the time. Inserting the 5th gives you a steady flow of time. Play shell to the 5th in your left hand, and the melody in your right hand.

Time Signature: This piece is in 3/4 time, 3 beats per measure. I suggest that you play this tune with the shell to the 5th on beats 1 and 3. You could also do beats 1 and 2, but I find 1 and 3 to be more relaxing.

Slash Chords: There are a few slash chords in this piece, and I don't cover this until Week 3. If you are here earlier, play the note to the right of the slash with your pinky and thumb, an octave apart, to create the shell. Play the note to the left of the slash on beat 3 as if you were playing the 5th. For example, for C/E play two Es an octave apart and on beat 3 play the C with your index finger.

Augmented Chords: There is a Caug and a Faug. Play the root–octave as the shell and play a ♯5th as the 5th.

Pedaling: Remember your pedaling, up and then down at the start of each chord. This allows you to hear all three tones of the chord together, while giving you an opportunity to reposition your left hand after playing the 5th on beat 3. An entire beat+ to get in position for the next chord.

Chord Isolation: If you are having difficulty playing the left hand smoothly, try chord isolation at the start. With chord isolation, you ignore most of the melody in the right hand and instead play only the note under the chord. This allows you to concentrate more on your left hand. As you get comfortable, you can move up to the full melody.

Base Patterns

4 Patterns: You have four patterns to choose from, 1–5–octave, 1–5–7, 1–5–10, and 1–7–10. Start with 1–5–octave and work your way up as you are comfortable.

Adjust for Chord Type: This piece challenges your understanding of how to adjust for various chord types, so you may want to delay this base-patterns portion until week 6. Here is the list of adjustments:

- **aug:** 1–♯5–octave, or 1–♯5–10
- **6:** 1–5–octave, 1–5–6, 1–5–10, or 1–6–10
- **dom7:** 1–5–octave, 1–5–♭7, 1–5–10, 1–♭7–10
- **min7:** 1–5–octave, 1–5–♭7, 1–5–♭10, 1–♭7–♭10
- **dim7:** 1–♭5–octave, 1–♭5–♭♭7, 1–♭5–♭10, or 1–♭♭7–♭10
- **slash:** bass-root chord-root bass-octave (e.g., C/E plays as E C E)

Watch the Video: In this piece, there are so many adjustments that you should definitely watch the video at www.pianoinstruction.com to learn how I look at a piece and adjust and possibly notate my adjustments.

Play Low in the Left?: When playing these patterns, especially the ones with a big spread to the 10th, you can play them an octave lower to keep your hands from colliding. Patterns lend themselves to playing low; the individual notes sound very nice. You can adjust your pattern selection to a pattern within the octave range. Get used to adjusting from the octave range to the 10th selections.

3rds on Compression

My Favorite Combination: This option shows my favorite style, shell to the 5th in my left hand and 3rds on compression in my right hand. Make sure you are good with shells to the 5th and melody before moving up to this style. I start showing you 3rds on compression in Week 2; it is best to wait until then, and perhaps even Week 3 or 4.

Keep It Slow: Your right hand has so much to do that keeping the pace slow will lend itself to a more relaxed presentation of the music.

2 Chords per Bar: Remember the piece is in 3/4 time. Only 3 beats to use. Try either a shell (easy) or shell to the 5th on beats 1 and 2 for the 1st chord, and a shell on beat 3 for the 2nd chord. Remember to play a 3rd at the compression of each of the chords.

Chord Isolation: You can do chord isolation if you are having problems here. With chord isolation, you ignore most of the melody in the right hand and instead play only the note under the chord. In this case, however, you need to add the 3rd below the melody note as well.

My Wild Irish Rose

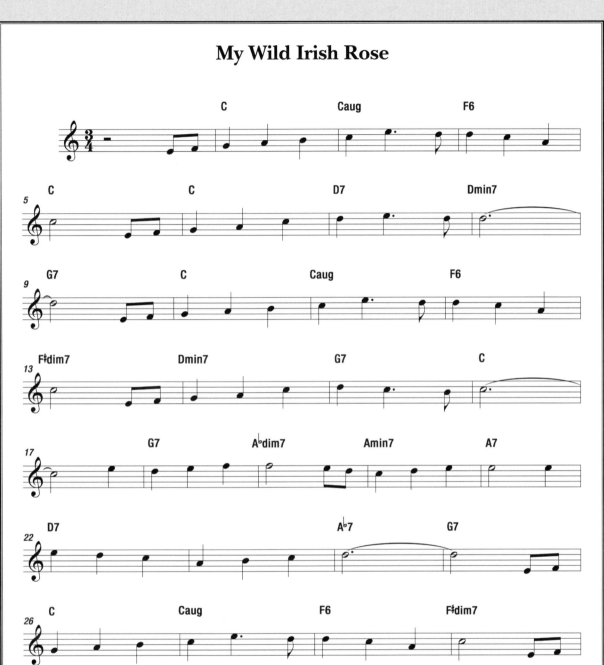

My Wild Irish Rose

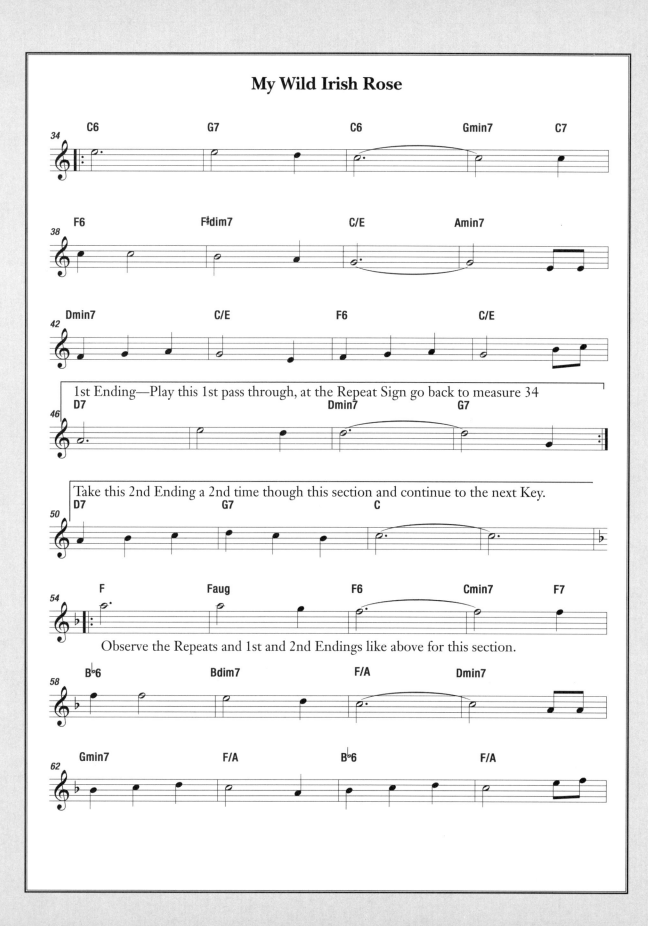

My Wild Irish Rose

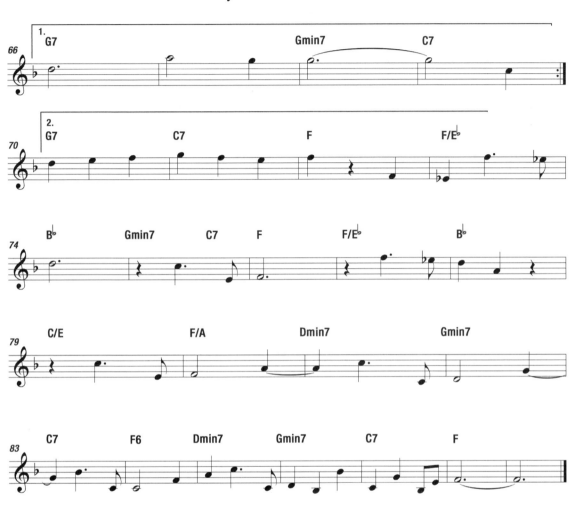

Back Home in Indiana

Choose a playing option that you are comfortable with today.

Videos

Back Home in Indiana: Back Home in Indiana with shells and melody
Back Home in Indiana: Back Home in Indiana with shell to the 5th and melody
Back Home in Indiana: Back Home in Indiana with base patterns applied
Back Home in Indiana: Back Home in Indiana with 3rds on compression

Watch the videos on www.pianoinstruction.com. You will gain insight on how to play the various options, the sound and tempo of the tune, and how to plan for every little issue that will come your way.

Shells

Play the 1–7 shells in your left hand and the melody in your right hand.

Key Signature: The key signature is the key of F, so all Bs are flat.

Travel with Pedal: Remember you're pedaling, up then down at each chord. The pedal will free your left hand early and allow you to travel to the upcoming shell, putting yourself in position a whole beat ahead of time.

Shells to the 5th

A Mainstay: Shell to the 5th is a very important skill; it is a mainstay of your playing that you will use all the time. Inserting the 5th gives you a steady flow of time. Play shell to the 5th in your left hand, and the melody in your right hand.

Two Chords per Bar: When you run across a bar with two chords, play a shell for each chord.

Slash Chords: There is a slash chord in this piece, and I don't cover this until Week 3. If you are here earlier, play the note to the right of the slash with your pinky and thumb, an octave apart to create the shell. Play just the shell, ignore the 5th. For Dm/C, play two Cs an octave apart.

Flat 5: The min7$^\flat$5 and dim7 chords have a $^\flat$5.

Pedaling: Remember your pedaling, up and down at the start of each chord. This allows you to carry the left hand selection while giving you an opportunity to reposition your left hand.

Chord Isolation: If you are having difficulty playing the left hand smoothly, try chord isolation at the start. With chord isolation, you ignore most of the melody in the right hand and instead play only the note under the chord. This allows you to concentrate more on your left hand. As you get comfortable, you can move up to the full melody.

Base Patterns

4 Patterns: You have four patterns to choose from, 1–5–octave, 1–5–7, 1–5–10, and 1–7–10. Start with 1–5–octave and work your way up as you are comfortable.

Adjust for Chord Type: Figure out your adjustments for chord type. The most difficult in this tune is the Bdim7 in bar 29, which has a ♭5, ♭♭7, and ♭10.

Keep it Low?: When playing these patterns, especially the ones with a big spread to the 10th, you can play your left hand an octave lower to keep your hands from colliding. Patterns lend themselves to playing low; the individual notes sound very nice. If, however, you are playing shells in your left hand, playing low tends to give you muddy sounds; move them up closer to your right hand.

3rds on Compression

My Favorite Combination: This option shows my favorite style, shell to the 5th in my left hand and 3rds on compression in my right hand. Make sure you are good with shells to the 5th and melody before moving up to this style. I start showing you 3rds on compression in Week 4; it is best to wait until at least then, if not even Week 5.

2 Chords per Bar: Use shells in the right hand when you find two chords per bar.

Adjust: Watch for the Bdim7. Figure out your adjustment beforehand.

Chord Isolation: You can do chord isolation if you are having problems here. With chord isolation, you ignore most of the melody in the right hand and instead play only the note under the chord. In this case, however, you need to add the 3rd below the melody note as well.

Back Home in Indiana

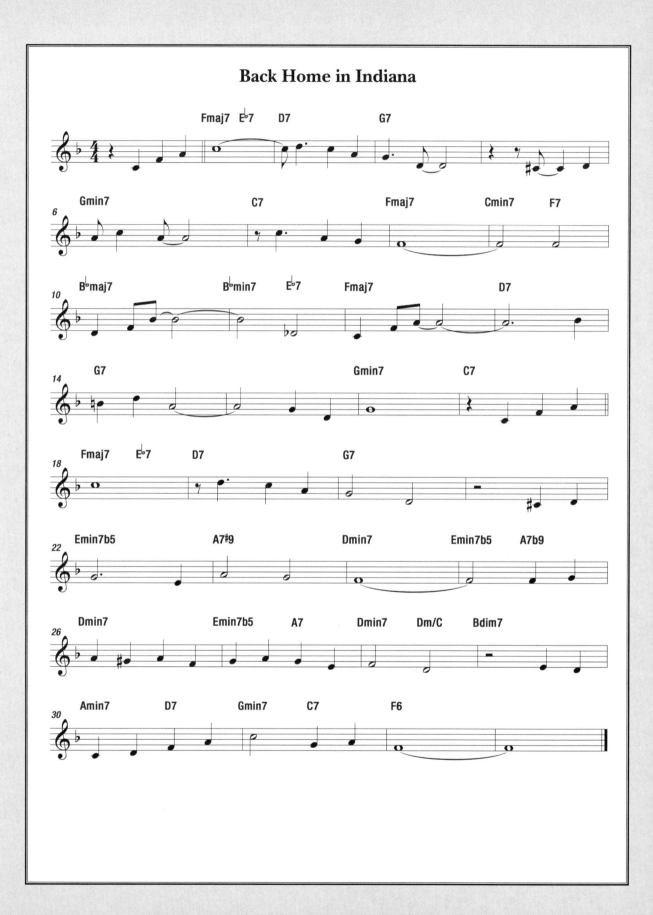

Happy Birthday

Choose a playing option that you are comfortable with today.

Videos

Happy Birthday: *Happy Birthday with shells and melody*

Happy Birthday: *Happy Birthday with shell to the 5th and melody*

Happy Birthday: *Happy Birthday with base patterns applied*

Happy Birthday: *Happy Birthday with 3rds on compression*

Watch the videos on www.pianoinstruction.com. You will gain insight on how to play the various options, the sound and tempo of the tune, and how to plan for every little issue that will come your way.

Shells

Play the 1–7 shells in your left hand and the melody in your right hand.

Key signature: We are in the key of F, so all B's are flat.

Time Signature: There are two different time signatures, 3/4 and 4/4 time.

Csus4: Decide what to do with this chord. I made a shell by playing a C and a C an octave higher.

Bounce Shell: After getting comfortable with the piece, try bouncing the shell to give it a little up-tempo.

Shells to the 5th

A Mainstay: Shell to the 5th is a very important skill; it is a mainstay of your playing that you will use all the time. Inserting the 5th gives you a steady flow of time. Play shell to the 5th in your left hand, and the melody in your right hand.

3/4 Time: Apply the shell on beat 1 and the 5th on beat 2. In those places where you have more than 1 chord per bar, play some shells.

4/4 Time: Play mostly shell to the 5th on the beat. If you end up with too much to do, revert to shells.

Csus4: I just played C7. Remember to look through your pieces to find those chords that you may have to adjust.

Base Patterns

4 Patterns: You have four patterns to choose from: 1–5–octave, 1–5–7, 1–5–10, and 1–7–10. Start with 1–5–octave and work your way up as you are comfortable.

3/4 Time: You can't play the full pattern all the time. If you only have 2 beats available, play the 1–5 or even the 1–10. Sometimes you only have 1 beat available; play the shell.

4/4 Time: Where you have enough beats, play the 3-note pattern. If you have only 2 beats, make up your own 2-beat pattern, either 1–5 or 1–10. Where you have only 1 beat, play the shell.

3rds on Compression

My Favorite Combination: This option shows my favorite style, shell to the 5th in my left hand and 3rds on compression in my right hand. Make sure you are good with shells to the 5th and melody before moving up to this style. I start showing you 3rds on compression in Week 4; it is best to wait until at least then, if not even Week 5.

3/4 Time: Apply the Shell on beat 1 and the 5th on beat 2. In those places where you have more than 1 chord per bar, play some shells.

4/4 Time: Play mostly shell to the 5th on the beat. If you end up with too much to do, revert to shells.

Csus4: The 3rd is not an available tone on a sus4 chord. Don't play a 3rd on compression for this chord.

Happy Birthday
3/4 and 4/4 Time

Shenandoah

Choose a playing option that you are comfortable with today.

Videos

Shenandoah: Shenandoah with shells and melody
Shenandoah: Shenandoah with shell to the 5th and melody
Shenandoah: Shenandoah with base patterns applied
Shenandoah: Shenandoah with 3rds on compression

Watch the videos on www.pianoinstruction.com. You will gain insight on how to play the various options, the sound and tempo of the tune, and how to plan for every little issue that will come your way.

Shells

Play the 1–7 shells in your left hand and the melody in your right hand.

Key Signature: The key signature is the key of C, no sharps or flats.

Chords Adjustment, Pencil in Adjustments: There a slash chord in this piece, and I don't cover this until Week 3. If you are here earlier, play the note to the right of the slash with your pinky and thumb, an octave apart to create the shell. For example, for C/E, play two Es an octave apart.

Sus and sus4 chords can be played using the root–octave of the chord. The Gsus4 followed by G7 in bars 4 and 14 can be played as a G7.

Shells to the 5th

A Mainstay: Shell to the 5th is a very important skill; it is a mainstay of your playing that you will use all the time. Inserting the 5th gives you a steady flow of time. Play shell to the 5th in your left hand, and the melody in your right hand.

Chords Adjustment, Pencil in Adjustments: I suggest these solutions. Pencil them in on your piece.

C/E play E C E	C play C G C (root—5—octave)	F/G play G F G
Cmaj7/A play A E A	Csus4 play C C (shell only)	

On the Beat: There are 2 chords per bar everywhere in this piece. Play your shell to the 5th on the beat: shell—5th—shell—5th on beat 1, 2, 3, 4.

Base Patterns

4 Patterns: You have four patterns to choose from, 1–5–octave, 1–5–7, 1–5–10, and 1–7–10. Start with 1–5–octave and work your way up as you are comfortable.

Chords Adjustment, Pencil in Adjustments: I suggest these solutions, same as in shell to the 5th. Pencil them in on your piece.

C/E play E C E	C play C G C (root—5—octave)	F/G play G F G
Cmaj7/A play A E A	Csus4 play C C (shell only)	

3rds on Compression

Be Familiar: Be familiar and comfortable with this piece before trying 3rds on compression; it is an intricate tune with a lot of chord changes. If you rush into it you will have trouble concentrating on the 3rds.

My Favorite Combination: This option shows my favorite style, shell to the 5th in my left hand and 3rds on compression in my right hand. Make sure you are good with shells to the 5th and melody before moving up to this style. I start showing you 3rds on compression in Week 4, it is best to wait at least until then, if not even Week 5.

Chord Adjustment: Use the adjustments penciled in for shell to the 5th.

Adjust: Gsus4, and any sus4, should play the 4th on compression, not the 3rd. The 4th is one note higher than the 3rd.

Bar 5 and Others: The Amin7 in bar 5 is compressed without any new note below it in the right hand. Add the 3rd in the right hand, played along with the chord compression. Similar situations occur throughout the tune, for example bars 7, 9, 11, 13, etc.

Slash Chords: Here is a tip on finding the 3rd for slash chords. A slash chord has the format F/G or chord/bass-note. When you are looking for the 3rd, choose the 3rd of the chord. Thus in F/G, the 3rd would be the 3rd of the F chord. Cmaj7/A would use the 3rd of the Cmaj7 chord.

Fragment: There is a lot of music to play in this tune. Do a few bars or a line at a time and get comfortable.

Chord Isolation: You can do chord isolation if you are having problems here. With chord isolation, you ignore most of the melody in the right hand and instead play only the note under the chord. In this case, however, you need to add the 3rd below the melody note as well.

Shenandoah

Shenandoah

The Final Word: Where You Are and Where You Can Go

We have come to the end of our book. The only thing left is to apply your skills to tunes and to become more comfortable with the skills while having some fun. These techniques will become second nature the more you apply them. Use the tunes supplied with the book or use some of your own favorites. Go out and get some fake books or lead sheets; you should be ready to play them with a new level of technique and sound. Have some fun.

The six weeks of this book have brought you to a very exciting level in your playing. It's a set of skills that you can enjoy forever, and it can be a foundation for other enjoyable techniques.

The core of this book is learning to take the chords of your tunes and creatively mix them in with the melodies. You have learned how to find the chord tones (root, 3rd, 5th, 7th along with the octave, and 10th), adjust them for all chord types, and apply them to your melodies with numerous techniques (root, shell, shell to the 5th, 3-note and 2-note patterns, stride, pulsing). Most exciting of all, you have learned how to start spreading your chords across both hands, using 3rds on compression and 3rds as an inner tonal movement.

You can take this core and create beautiful music forever; it by itself is a fantastic place to be. You can build on this foundation, learning more techniques to spread the available tones of the chord between both hands. You can move into improvisation by learning techniques to utilize the chord tones and tensions freely in your playing. I have also exposed you to the blues and diatonic improvisation. You can explore either of these areas more in the future.

I would like to wrap up by outlining where we are in each of our skill tracks, and where you can go when you choose to progress beyond where we are now.

Shells

Shells are the most powerful professional tool you will ever use. In the shells lessons, you have learned a fast effective means to play all chords on a piano.

What you have learned:
- The 4 chord tones.
- Modifying the chord tones to fit all chord types.
- Using the shell to the 5th to establish time on the piano.
- Spreading the chord tones across two hands.

In the future, you can explore:
- Advanced chordal harmonies as you continue to spread the available tones of the chord between your hands with additional techniques.
- Create pattern options from the core shell.
- Advanced stride skills.

Shells to the 5th

Shells to the 5th has given you a wonderful inner tonal movement element in your left hand that both frames the chord and uses a chord tone to provide time to your playing. This is a very important core skill for you now and in the future.

What you have learned:

- Playing shells to the 5th: playing the shell and adding the 5th as an inner total movement.

In the future, you can explore:

- Advanced use of other available tones as tonal movement elements in your right hand.
- Developing stride, patterns, and bass lines from this core shape.

Diatonic Improvisation

Diatonic improvisation has given you a simple and safe arena to explore freeform right hand movement all over the keyboard. In the end, it was integrated with all the other techniques you learned in the book to give you the right-hand freeform coupled with the various left-hand techniques. A fun place to play.

What you have learned:

- A simple and safe way of exploring right-hand improvisational playing while playing 3-note chordal patterns in your left hand.
- Key notes that work well with each of the 7 patterns.
- Void notes that must be resolved for each of the seven patterns.
- Creating textures for an advanced sound in your playing.

In the future, you can explore:

- Diatonic patterns will move seamlessly into all of your pattern playing.
- Use these diatonic skills in all keys, not just the key of C.
- Create beautiful diatonic introductions and endings using this skill in all keys.

Patterns

In patterns, you have learned how to create left-hand patterns using the four chord tones, modifying the chord tones to adjust for all chords. These patterns let the left hand create the time for the music.

What you have learned:

- Four different 3-note patterns.
- Adjusting the pattern notes for all chord types.
- Mixing the patterns in with shells and shell to the 5th.
- Using patterns to define the chord while keeping time.

In the future you can explore:

- Extend the four base patterns to many more options.
- Use the patterns as a chordal foundation while developing right-hand improvisational ideas, and much more.

Stride

In stride, you have learned another left-hand technique for maj7, dom7, and min7 chords, giving you open chordal support for your left hand.

What you have learned:

- The base stride technique (root to 7–10) for maj7, dom7, and min7 chords.
- Combining stride with shell to the 5th.

In the future, you can explore:

- Variations on the base stride technique.
- Wide and narrow textures in your stride playing.
- How to chromatically set up and feed the upcoming chords.

3rds on Compression

3rds on compression is a powerful technique that starts the spread of the chord tones into the right hand. It generates a full, rich sound in your playing.

What you have learned:

- How to find the 3rd and ♭3rd, and the chords that they appear in.
- Incorporating the 3rd into the melody in your right hand by adding it on compression of the chord.

In the future, you can explore:

- Additional inner tonal movements of the 3rd, as well as the inner tonal movement of other available tones.

Inner Tonal Movement

What you have learned:

- The power of movement in your left hand using the 5th as a tonal move helps keep time in your playing.
- The power of moving the 3rd into your right hand, inserting it at appropriate moments.

In the future, you can explore:

- A deep systematic look into how the placement of tones will add not only to the overall sound but will establish movement to keep the sound, keeping time in your playing.
- Inner tonal movement will have you trained to be searching for creative places to move tones as we progress into higher levels, adding more tones and seeing all the options.

Blues

What you have learned:

- In blues, you have learned how to apply our left-hand techniques to blues tunes.
- You have explored blues improvisation with the C blues scale.

In the future, you can explore: playing blues in other keys, chordal structures built on chords, moving beyond the blues scale, a variety of blues progressions, and more.

Appendices

Appendix A: Shells

The Shell is one of the most exciting and game-changing techniques of my method, a skill that will become the foundation of your playing forever.

The Video: *Appendix: Shells Master*

What Is a Shell?

A shell is the outer edges of a chord. Through the use of three simple formulas, you will be able to find the outer edges of any and all chords after only a few minutes of practice. After a few days, this will be automatic. Just think, you will be able to pick up a tune in any key, with any chord types, and play it right away without scratching your head about how to play any given chord. It is a fast, professional way to get up and going. It is a game changer.

The Power of the Shell Foundation

Using the shell as a foundation, you can then learn the chord tones that represent the inner portions of the chord. With the shell as the left-hand foundation, these chord tones can be spread out into both hands, the left and the right, to give professional qualities to your playing.

Whereas the shell is typically the 1 and the 7, the inner chord tones of the 3 and the 5 and their siblings like the 10th fill out the chord and give the tonal nuances. Using the shell, you will be able to add a tone like the 5th into the left hand for the rhythmic shell to the 5th or 3-note patterns. And using the shell, you will be able to add the chord tones to your right hand for textured harmonization, or even freeform improvisation.

It all starts with these three little formulas:

1 note down for the maj7

2 notes down for the min7, min7♭5, dom7, aug7

3 notes down for the maj6, min6, dim7

Learn how to find shells and change your playing forever by going through the exercise sheet on the following page.

Free Videos

Remember to watch the video for the shells from my website, www.pianoinstruction.com. The videos are free; you just need to register with your email, and they are easier than reading some instructions, and they are unbelievably informative. The Appendix portion of the videos is at the end of the list of videos on the video page.

Shells
Master Application

Shells are one the most important and powerful skills you can learn as you enter Chord playing application. They are brought to you here in three simple, easy-to-follow formulas that will have you learning most chords on the piano very quickly. Please note there are several ways to display the notation of each chord.

The Shell—The outer edge of the chord. Play the 3 through all keys—Left Hand

One Note Down From Octave—This first formula in Left Hand will have you playing the outer edges of the Major7 chord.

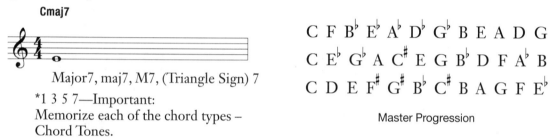

Cmaj7

Major7, maj7, M7, (Triangle Sign) 7

*1 3 5 7—Important:
Memorize each of the chord types –
Chord Tones.

C F B♭ E♭ A♭ D♭ G♭ B E A D G
C E♭ G♭ A C♯ E G B♭ D F A♭ B
C D E F♯ G♯ B♭ C♯ B A G F E♭

Master Progression

Two Notes Down From Octave—Here we step down 2 notes from the Octave to create 4 Chord Types.

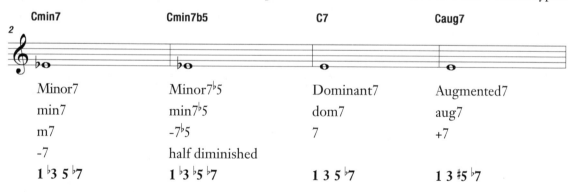

Cmin7	Cmin7b5	C7	Caug7
Minor7	Minor7♭5	Dominant7	Augmented7
min7	min7♭5	dom7	aug7
m7	-7♭5	7	+7
-7	half diminished		
1 ♭3 5 ♭7	1 ♭3 ♭5 ♭7	1 3 5 ♭7	1 3 ♯5 ♭7

Three Notes Down From Octave—Now we step down 3 notes from the Octave to create 3 Chord Types.

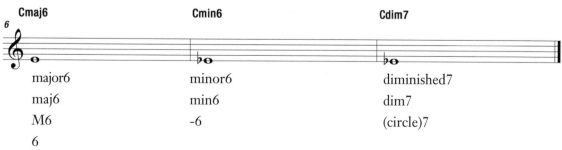

Cmaj6	Cmin6	Cdim7
major6	minor6	diminished7
maj6	min6	dim7
M6	-6	(circle)7
6		

Appendix B: Finding the 5th

Video: *Appendix: Reading Add the 5th*

The illustration on the right illustrates how to find every 5th. It's easy.

Take a look at C; the 5th and the root are 5 white keys apart.

For C#, the 5th and the root are 4 black keys apart.

This works for all notes (with one exception: see the next paragraph); if the root is a white key like a D, the 5th is also a white key, and they are five white keys apart. If the root is a black key, the 5th is also a black key, and they are 4 black keys apart.

There is an exception, and that is B and B♭ (or A#). For those two 2 keys, the 5th is a different color than the root; white root and black 5th, or black root and white 5th. Take a look at B and B♭ to see what I mean.

Play through these 5ths. They are easy to find; they all feel like the same separation. After a few minutes, you should start finding the 5th almost instantly.

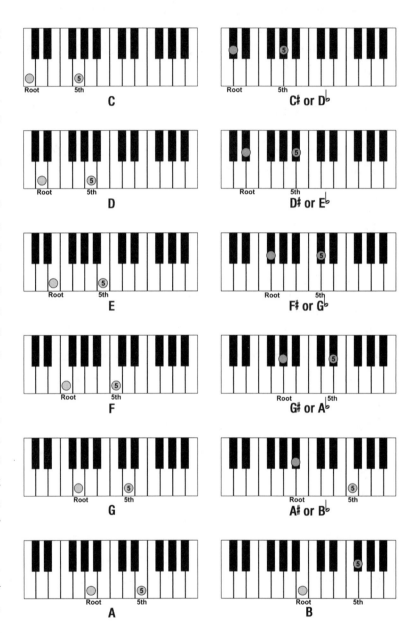

Appendix C: Counting

The following seven pages provide a substantial amount of information, illustrating our most commonly seen rhythms. This will help you build an effective professional foundation for your playing, both now and even at higher levels. I have attached practice sheets which also prompt you to play shells, or shells to the 5th, or even 3-note patterns in your left hand to accompany your right-hand counting exercises.

Free Videos

These exercises are always more effective with our free videos. The videos give you instruction, and they also let you know how the exercise should sound if you are playing it correctly. Find the videos at www.pianoinstruction.com. Just register with your email and you have access.

Held Options
(Root) (1, 7) (157)

Held Options will be the first part of what to do with the Shells you have now learned. We will at this time bring forth the element of Counting in 4/4 time, focusing on the Whole Note, Dotted Half Note, Half Note, and Quarter Note. It is important to understand that the Held Options must be understood first before Broken and Pattern Options can be applied.

Take the extra time here to count in 4/4 time (4 beats to a measure) the melodies here against the Left Hand Held Options. Be sure to be reading melodies regularly to gain more proficiency and play attention to the various note values.

Left Hand: Level 1–(Root)   Level 2–(1, 7)   Level 3–(157)

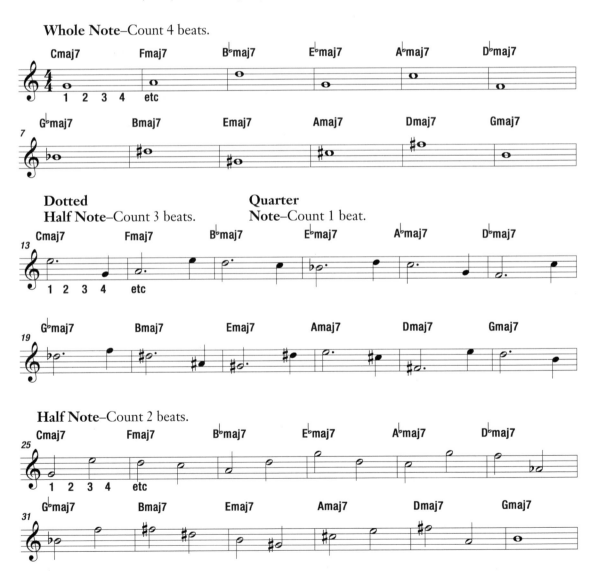

Held Options

Quarter Notes–1 beat each in 4/4 time.

We are focusing on the major7 Shell here to enable you to fully focus on the counting component in your playing now. These held options should be explored in your tunes and for sure once you are comfortable with these, you will be ready to add movement with the Broken variations and Patterns.

Important Things to Know:

1. Be comfortable playing the lower level of application before moving onto the more difficult ones.
2. Fingering—Use whatever fingering feels comfortable. Try to avoid using the same finger for 2 different notes.
3. Always be looking ahead as you read the melodies.
4. Double check the Key Signature and Time Signature for any and all tunes.
5. Be sure to fully understand the values of whole, dotted half, half, and quarter notes in 4/4.
6. When practicing, it is important to be playing your skills applied to all keys—like in these exercises to better prepare you for more advanced playing.

Practice means to be playing things you don't know!

Broken Options
(Root–7) (Shell–5th) (Root, 5th–7th)

Now that we are somewhat comfortable with the Shells, we will now begin the Broken Options. This will begin to add motion to your left hand, keeping steady time. It is very important to make sure you have full understanding of the Held Options before beginning these Broken Options.

We break down the Options in such a way that eventually any of them can be played and always be viewed as a professional skill.

Root—7th is the first Broken Option we play and itself just outlines the Shell. Very powerful in its own right.

Shell—5th is a powerful configuration of Left Hand movement. Emphasis on the Shell here and when the 5th is added, it provides a solid stable motion.

Root—5th to 7th is just a varied spin on the Root, 5, 7 that you find yourself using in conjunction with all the rest.

Count—Broken Options & Solid Placement

It is important to be counting to effectively place in the Broken Options. In this exercise we will be putting our focus on the steady even application on beats 1 and 3 in the Left Hand. By watching the counting below carefully, you can see how they are placed. We also are mainly playing maj7 chords to enable you to put all energy into counting RH.

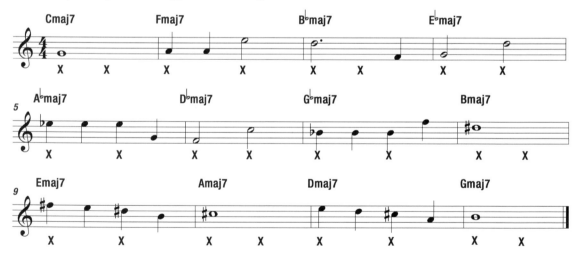

Take time to find measures of music and attempt to play Broken Options. You may in the beginning stages place markings as to where the 1 and 3 are in the bar but soon do your best to avoid doing this.

There are other forms of Inner Tonal Movement that I teach that will have you placing tones on every beat. Get control of this stable 1 and 3 and will help more advanced application.

The Rest

The Rest is a very important part of our counting and it will hold great value as you will see it provides the pace, we so like to input valuable tones in our playing that helps keep time. Here is a quick viewing of the Quarter Rest, which in 4/4 time will receive 1 beat rest and the Half Rest which sits on the 3rd line and will rest for 2 beats. The Whole Rest will look like the half rest however it hangs from the 4th lines.

Quarter Rest   Half Rest   Whole Rest

Right Hand—Count very carefully 4 beats to a measure.

Left Hand—Play each of the Held Position (Root) (Shell) (157) and the Broken Position. (Root–7th) (Shell–5th) (15–7) on beats 1 and 3.

Quarter Note Rest

Half Note Rest

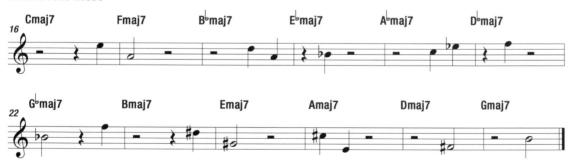

Important: Work through some bars of music and pay attention to counting the melody to help control the Left Hand correct positioning on beats 1 and 3.

There are other forms of Inner Tonal Movements that I will be teaching however it is important to understand Beat 1 and 3 and its values.

The "Tie"

The Tie is a line that connects 2 notes or more that appear on the same line. When you see a tie, you add the value of the combined notes holding the note down.

Often you will see the Tie used to separate the bar halfway so visually it is easier to play, as shown here in the example. When you Tie the 2 quarter notes, it could be notated as a half note like on the 2nd measure. The more you count and read, the more you will see that being able to visually see the measure in half is very helpful.

Apply yourself below and set your Left Hand to provide a challenging level to support your Right Hand melody reading.

Tie—Workpiece

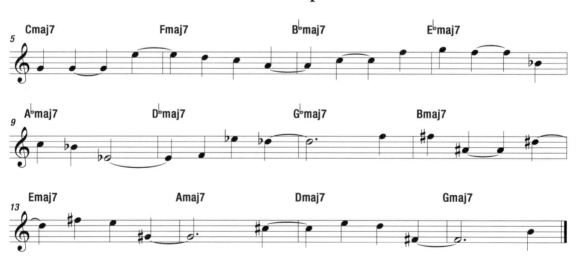

Left Hand Levels

Left Hand: Held	Left Hand: Broken	Left Hand: Patterns
1. Root Alone	1. Root to 7	1. 1—5—Octave
2. 1, 7 Held	2. Shell to 5th	2. 1—5—7
3. 157 Held	3. Root, 5th to 7th	3. 1—7—5
		*1 5 10 (advanced)

Tie & Rest
Worktune

The Tie and the Rest will often add some complexity to your overall melody reading. Be careful to count carefully and adjust your Left Hand to set a challenge as you work through this melody.

It is important to find measures of music and work out your counting each bar to be better prepared. We will eventually be covering other time signatures. However, for now it is best to feel comfortable counting in 4/4 time.

Left Hand: Minor7 Focus Options

Held	**Broken**	**Patterns**
1. Root Alone	1. Root to 7	1. 1—5—Octave
2. 1, 7 Held	2. Shell to 5th	2. 1—5—7
3. 157 Held	3. Root, 5th to 7th	3. 1—7—5
		*1 5 10 (advanced)

Worktune

Apply LH Options!

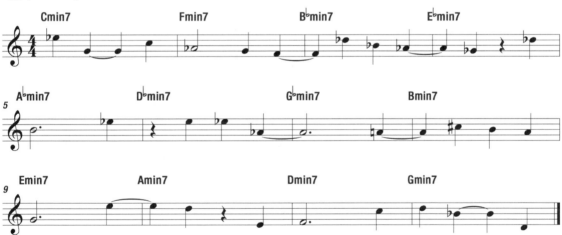

Important: Try to apply yourself with a variety of Left Hand Support while you count the melody.

In this Worktune, we kept the melody simple with lots of Quarter Notes present and strong focus on the Minor7th Left Hand. So this will serve you well for gaining more skill in your Left Hand as you learn to navigate through a melody with ties. You will see just how important the Left Hand is to keep stable and consistent when you are counting your melodies.

The Eighth Note

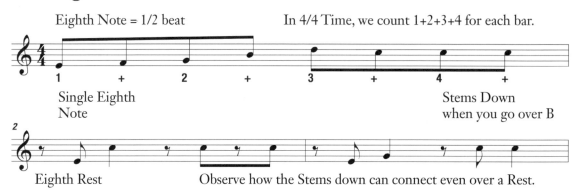

Important: Observe the Halfway mark in the measure. It is very important to be able to see the bars of music in 2-beat half sections.

Left Hand: Held	**Left Hand:** Broken	**Left Hand:** Patterns
1. Root Alone	1. Root to 7	1. 1–5–Octave
2. 1, 7 Held	2. Shell to 5th	2. 1–5–7
3. 157 Held	3. Root, 5th to 7th	3. 1–7–5
		*1–5–10 (advanced)

Eighth Note Introduction – Worktune

Appendix D: Scales

The following five pages show you how to play white-key scales, black-key scales, major 7th scales, and scales for many octaves.

There is a lot of practicing that you could do here.

To succeed in this book, it is not absolutely necessary to be totally comfortable playing all your scales. You probably can move on to the other parts of the book right now. But scales are good practice, as they build good hand technique, as well as getting you to see the inner chord parts of each key. Scales are ultimately an essential part of one's practice when moving to higher levels of playing. So you should come back here every once in a while and run through some scales.

Free Videos

The best way to see, hear, and learn about scales is to watch the videos on my website www. pianoinstruction.com. Use the following exercise pages along with the videos. The videos are high quality, extremely informative, and free. I have been delivering videos for over 30 years, and I am the pioneer of video-based piano instruction, all the way back to the time when I supplied videos on the now obsolete Betamax format. Just come to the site and register with your email address.

Scales–White Keys
1 Octave—Hands Separate

C G D A E

Right Hand: 1 2 3 1 2 3 4 5
Left Hand: 5 4 3 2 1 3 2 1
*These 5 scales share the exact same fingering.

B and F Scale have alterations in the fingering, so be careful.

Scales–Black Keys
Traditional Fingering
1 Octave—Separate

Here we focus on the Black Key Scales applying our Traditional Fingering. Pay extra attention to the Thumb Pivoting Points on the B–C or E–F. This will help you effectively move through these 5 Black Key Scales.

Remember the White Keys

It is important while focusing on the Black Key Scales to be continually playing the White Keys with firm accurate control of both hands separate.

Black Key Scales

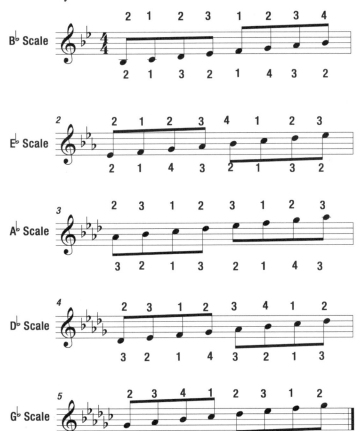

Important: It is important to understand the Key Signature that is associated with each scale.

Play each scale with Both Hands Separate paying extra attention to the Thumb Pivoting locations within the scale.

It is effective to be taking one scale at a time and work each hand with the correct fingering.

Smooth and even application is your goal here. Keep temp slow as you ascend and descend.

Major Scale
Breakdown–1 Octave–Hands Separate

3–4–5–6–7 (Note Breakdown)

It is through this process you will become more intimate with the Major scale and have much more control. By breaking the practice into small fragments where you play the scale not in its octave range, it will help you pay attention to the ending Degree. Play each scale with Both Hands Separate paying extra attention to the Thumb Pivoting locations within the scale.

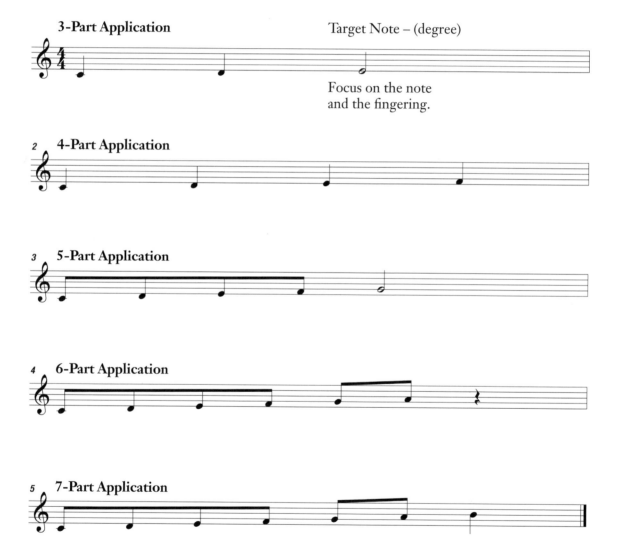

Scales—All Keys
Traditional Fingering
2 Octaves

Scales–All Keys
2 Octaves

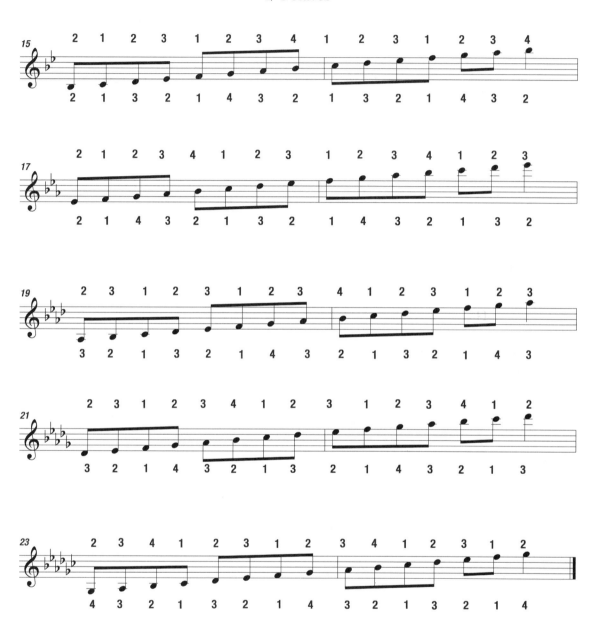

Important: Use the fingering on these pages for reference only. Practice the scales with no fingering listed. Observe the fingering to each scale and put to memory.

Index

About the Authors

Bill Chotkowski

Bill Chotkowski is a graduate of the Massachusetts Institute of Technology, receiving a BSAD (Bachelor of Science in Art and Design) while studying computer graphics when computer graphics was in its infancy. MIT was trying understand this emerging field and invented the BSAD degree for Bill and used him as one of their test cases for their computer graphics direction in the future. This means that not only did Bill receive a cutting edge computer education, but he also received the first computer art degree ever given out by MIT.

From digital imaging, to icons on your desktops, to the availability of documents worldwide, Bill has been influential in the development of the things that you use every day on your PC. Because his career has been delivering solutions in new metaphors, he has learned to understand people and how they perceive and understand the world about them. Bill uses these skills to deliver products and concepts to people that are easily understood and utilized.

Recently Bill has been publishing personal instruction titles, both electronically and paper-based, with the same level of fun and ingenuity that he has brought to computers.

Dan Delaney

Originally from Boston, now residing in Cave Creek, AZ, is a highly regarded pianist, entrepreneur, author, artist for Earthworks Professional Microphone Systems and a dedicated and innovative teacher of the piano, jazz improvisation, and harmony.

Dan attended the Berklee College of Music back in 1975 and quickly gained respect as a performer and teacher in Boston for many years. At that time, he developed his Personalized Video Correspondence, a video correspondence teaching technique that Keyboard Magazine and others acknowledged as a groundbreaking innovation in piano education.

Through the years Dan has had a very exciting life with his music and has created musical connections spanning the US having lived on the East coast to the West Coast. He supports his entrepreneurial side with regularly scheduled performances, lectures, new books, and other musical endeavors.

Currently Dan continues to teach students worldwide that wish to study with him via his Personalized Video Correspondence. His method of teaching has proven through the years to be a convenient, effective, and affordable way to provide high level instruction to students anywhere. More information to study personally with Dan can be found on his website.